Copyright © 2017 by Eco Asylum

All rights reserved. No part of this publication may be reproduced, distributed, or transmitted in any form or by any means, including photocopying, recording, or other electronic or mechanical methods, without the prior written permission of the publisher, except in the case of brief quotations embodied in critical reviews and certain other noncommercial uses permitted by copyright law. For permission requests, write to the publisher, addressed "Attention: Permissions Coordinator," at the address below.

Eco Asylum
1 St Paul St, Suite 303A
St Catharines, ON
L2R7L4
(289)929-6158
Ordering Information:
Quantity sales. Special discounts are available on quantity purchases by corporations, associations, and others. For details, contact the publisher at the address above.

Orders by U.S. trade bookstores and wholesalers. Please contact Eco Asylum:
Tel: (289) 929-6158 or www.ecoasylum.com

Schools and Libraries: Please contact Eco Asylum tel (289) 929-6158 or fill out the contact form at www.ecoasylum.com

Printed simultaneously in Canada and the United States of America. For translations, transcriptions, audio books and braile please fill out the contact form at www.ecoasylum.com

This novel is a work of fiction and entirely the construction of the author. Any resemblance to persons living or dead is entirely co-incidental.

chase the cat

HOW TO GET THE RELATIONSHIP <u>YOU</u> WANT

why this book? why now?

You're no dummy, and you need all of the facts. If you're familiar with the Player vs. Player series of books, you know that we give it to you straight. We pit the experts against eachother at the top of their game, to find out who would win in an epic battle of minds!

This book is about relationships. It was edited by Eco Asylum based on conversations with the people you love to hate. That guy who gets every girl, and you have no idea why. That girl who tames bad boys. Names have been changed to protect the not-so-innocent.

We sat at a table with these jerks and asked them one question: How do you do it?

Part One will tell you how to connect with people in a disconnected world, how to change your perspective and make yourself the most dateable person in the room, and how to navigate "the rules" in our time.

If you end up with too many dates this Friday, don't blame us.....

-Eco Asylum.

PART ONE

**FINDING "THE ONE"
(WITHOUT LOSING A KIDNEY TO THE BLACK MARKET)**

**"GOOD NIGHT!
GOOD NIGHT!
PARTING IS SUCH SWEET SORROW!**

**THAT I SHOULD SAY GOODNIGHT
TIL IT BE MORROW"
-JULIET**

**"NO-ONE WILL EVER BE BETTER THAN ROSELINE"
-ROMEO**

1
THE PERFECT PERSON FOR <u>YOU</u>

The gloves were on, and the players were standing in our favorite boxing gym, hitting the bag. They agreed that men and women seem to have very different goals when they search for "the one"....but as the conversation continued, they realized the answers weren't as obvious as male and female.

Here's what they had to say:

Ben: "Women say they want you for your great personality and all these reasons, but they aren't dating slobs."

Kayla: "Guys assume we only want long term relationships. Sometimes I just want to bang one out. But I don't want to have to SAY it."

Kyle: "A lot of guys are looking for long term relationships, too. They just don't want to have to SAY it."

Ben: "Yeah, well you're not."

Kyle (laughs): "I'm not. But some guys..."

It's hard to meet the right person when you don't know who that is. How can you find the perfect person when you have no idea what "perfect" means? It definitely means something different for you than it does for anyone else you know.

Players know that dating is a numers game, and the numbers don't always add up. Why? Because most of us are chasing the same thing.

We've all petted a stray cat in our lifetimes. Let's picture that adorable kitty cat, sitting on somebody's lawn, wearing some little collar that makes us really want to pet him. There are a number of other cats around, but this one is the fluffiest.

There are four of our friends with us, and you know what? We might have petted some other cat, except that our friends keep talking about THAT one, and how fluffy it is. Now it's a competition.

Maybe one of our friends is taller. One is faster. One has a better job and makes more money. If we can just beat them in a race to THAT cat, we're going to totally WIN IN LIFE and EVERYBODY'S GOING TO BE

JEALOUS.

What happens? We run. We chase that pussy down, our friends start running just as fast to catch it, and any cat with sense sees a crowd of people running toward it and bolts. Nobody catches it.

Worst of all, every other cat within a twenty block radius has run off and we're left, sad and alone, stuffing our hands in our pockets and wishing we had a cat. Any cat.

Maybe we console ourselves by joking with our friends about the cat who got away. Once in awhile, we even catch the cat.

That's when we realize that it wasn't really that fluffy. It wasn't really that soft. It was just something OTHER PEOPLE WANTED and we, of course, had to have it.

It was so stupid. There are twice as many cats on that street as there are people... maybe three times as many! What was going through our heads?

Ben: "You always want what you can't have."

Kyle: "I'm addicted to what I can't have.

What's the solution? Stop chasing the cat, and start chasing the cats. Find the perfect person for you. Not the perfect person for Vin Diesel or Paris Hilton or Sports Illustrated or Cosmo, the perfect person for YOU. Chances are, you've already met that person. Pieces of that person, anyway.

Let's put this puzzle together!

First, write down the names of every person of the appropriate gender, who you have ever met. Straight guys, that's every girl you've ever met. Lesbian women, that's every girl you've ever met.

It's important to include friends and family members. If your list includes only people you're attracted to sexually, there's no way we'll ever see a pattern here. Put away the part of you that just wants to get a little something for a minute, and consider the personalities of the people you know.

This might take a while. I'll wait....

When you're done, your list might look something like Kyle's.....

Kyle's was too long. Your list might look something like Kayla's:

dad brother uncle jeff greg joe blaise craig my ex ex 2 chilton ben kyle

Once you've made a list of every guy, girl, or transperson you know well, you're going to make another list. This may seem arbitrary, but it's important.

Making a list puts what you're thinking right in front of you. It helps you to visualize your thought process, and essentially "fake" the thought process of someone who has every cat in the neighborhood eating out of their hand.

Sounds good? Let's get on it.

Your next assignment is to make three lists of TRAITS. Think about the people you listed and ask yourself: What do I like about these people? What reminds me of myself? What can't I stand?

Ben: "Nothing you want is ever easy."

Kayla: "That's what he said."

Shannon: "Speak for yourself."

The Eye-Opening (and hilarious) case study that taught Ben why knowing what you want in a person, not just a bra size, is so important:

When I was a young guy in my twenties, it was hard to be taken seriously by women. Most of the girls I knew were very sexually experienced. I was thin, short, and they were all into jocks. To make matters worse, whenever I tried talking to a girl, my stutter took over and made me look like an i-i-i-idiot.

I was out at the bar one night when I met the "perfect" woman. She said all of the right things. She told me how attractive I was, complimented me on my intelligence instead of talking about how my friend was so muscular, and said my stutter was incredibly cute.

Wow! No girl had ever walked up and just started talking to ME. Usually, they laughed at me with their friends or ignored me completely. When she asked me to go home with her right then and there, I was like, oh man! Score! I felt like I had pretty much won the lottery at that point.

The smoking hot chick wants to go home with me? There's tons of guys who have been hitting on her all night and she wants to go home with me? It's pretty nice. That's a pretty good feeling.

So I went home with her.

(*Kyle: The guys are already laughing because they know what's going to happen.*)

She had said a couple times that she couldn't wait to get back to her place and do me. Looking back on it, that has a whole different meaning now. She told me to make myself comfortable and went into the bathroom. I laid down on the bed with my eyes closed.

And then, she came back in and straddled me. All I feel is this THUD, right in the middle of my chest. She was this HOT girl... still...but she had a dick. I mean, and it was BIG. I ran out the door into the hall with a t-shirt over my crotch. I didn't even get dressed. Of course, all her neighbors knew which apartment I had come from.

Your dating fails may not be as extreme as Ben's, but we're willing to bet you've got a list too. For these, we have provided you with this handy "fail graveyard", where you can put all of your embarassments and screw-ups to rest before reading on. Goodbye, telling your crush you like him in front of his girlfriend. Goodbye, blowing off the chick who came back incredibly hot a month later. Put them here and forget them. Nobody's going to judge you if you burn this page.

fail graveyard

Here lies your screwup.

Now that your fails are dead (and we can't say that we miss them), take a look at those three lists you made. What do you notice?

Did you notice that the things you like about the people in your life are similar? That the things you can't stand are pretty similar, too?

The most important thing to notice is that you're starting to think about the poeple you date as human beings. Congratulations.

Those traits on your "like" list form the perfect person for <u>you.</u>

The perfect person for you isn't about a body type, or a hair color, or any other physical trait. It's not even about finding someone who is the same as you are in every way. It's about finding someone with the traits you love in other people, whether that's a strong work ethnic, humanitarian spirit, or great fashion sense.

Kyle: I swipe right on every girl.

Ben: Exactly. That's what works. You talk to everyone. You don't exclude people because of some ideal in your head that doesn't match anybody in reality.

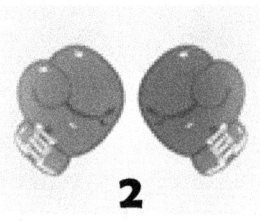

2

PEOPLE ARE NOT PRODUCTS

Have you ever bought a pet from a pet store? Fluffy little kittens in adorable enclosures full of toys, cat castles, and the cutest little ear-bows you can imagine?

Looking at these adorable, pure bred little muffin cakes you realize that even the cutest, fluffiest cat in your neighborhood pales in comparison to those pet store cuties in their glass enclosures, packaged not-at-all accidentally with tons of merchandise you just can't wait to buy for them.

To make matters worse for you, the glass enclosure is surrounded by total strangers who also think this is the cutest little thing they've ever seen in their lives. They're boochie-boochieing at the cat and giving it little names.

Kyle: "Celebrities would look like normal girls if you hadn't seen them on TV."

Shannon: "It's true. A guy can be completely unattractive, but if he's in a movie? Wow!"

What you need to realize about celebrities is what pet store employees realize when they are at home with their feet up, drowning their sorrows in Netflix binges and tossing smarties into their popcorn bag.

Some "people" are really just products.

The people you see on television, magazine covers, and movies are not real. They are constructed by an industry that exists to sell a product or lifestyle to you.

Even on social media sites, models are hired to create fake "ordinary person" posts that may confuse you into thinking real people act, talk, or look the way they do. The studios are the same, and so are the makeup artists.

Kyle: "I know what somebody's going to say, though. They're going to be like, no way. That chick really is that hot."

Shannon: "Guys always think we're jealous, when we're just trying to tell them that we're human. I'm human, she's human. Get over it. Like, why do you have to tell me who I'm not? Don't compare me to something fake."

Famous people endure a lot of pressure to

look a certain way, and even they crack under the pressure on occasion.

Everybody is human, and everybody has "problems" compared to the characters we see in movies and on television. Our players agreed that getting the date is about keeping their hangups to themselves.

Kayla: "I used to get in my own way a lot by not giving people a chance."

Ben: "Yeah. Some guys I know have read a lot of comic books, but they haven't met any girls."

Shannon: "To be fair, if some guy saved my life, I'd probably make out with him, too."

Kyle: "I'd make out with him!"

Walking into the back room of a pet store tells a whole different story from the one at the front. The little kittens we see through glass are switched out throughout the day. Out of ten or twenty kittens, only two or three will be placed in the glass enclosure, and only for an hour at a time.

It's so they don't pee in front of you.

Likewise, human celebrities have people who make sure that they never jeopardize their brand. Their personal lives are heavily guarded, and their personas are heavily managed.

Characters in the media are written for a very specific target market. Movies for men are full of beautiful young girls who would love to sleep with any of the three men at a giant party they can put their hands on, harems full of girls who just stand there saying nothing.

Women's movies are full of young, sensitive guys who are willing to date a much less attractive woman and would be happy to be with any girl in the world, as long as her personality was good enough.

Neither is realistic, but our fantasies don't have to be realistic. There's no harm as long as we realize that real people are not walking dolls. Nobody is your favorite character, not even the actor who plays him or her.

Ben: "I can't remember the last time I sparkled."
Kyle: "....or waited five years for some random girl to notice you."

the Completely Insane case study that taught Kayla why having "a high standard" isn't always a good thing.

I went to college, but some of my friends dropped out of high school to get married. I kept in touch with all of them, but I didn't really think about what married life was like.

Back then, I used to have a pretty good idea of the kind of guy I wanted to date. I'd sit around laughing about it with my friends. We'd just laugh off any guy who didn't meet our standard.

He had to be tall, for one thing. I'm 5'9 so there was no way I was going to date a guy who was shorter than me.

(Kyle: I'm right here.)

Unless he was extremely hot. Or famous. He also had to have a good job and a car. That was the minimum. Some of the guys I dated were students at my school but they all worked.

(Shannon: Or had a rich family.)

They all had money, one way or another. A

lot of guys complained about paying on dates, and I had no time for them.

One day, one of my friends who I had pretty much forgotten about called me crying. Her husband had just walked out on her. They got married when I started school, and I was in the middle of my Masters when they split up. Seven years.

At that time, the two of them had been with eachother longer than I had ever owned a pair of shoes. We were in our mid to late twenties, and he left my friend for a girl hardly out of her teens. She was completely heartbroken.

The worst thing about it was that she kept trying to reconcile. He finally gave it to her straight. He wasn't going back to her, and his reason was the most insane thing I have ever heard. He didn't want to date a woman with kids.

They were *his* kids.

He had this idea in his head of the perfect woman, but he didn't really think about himself as having any responsibility. He was like a kid in a playroom, grabbing toys.

Kyle: Okay, but he won.

Kayla: How?

Kyle: He got what he wanted. A younger girl who didn't have kids. Unless I'm missing something. Did she have kids?

Shannon: So that just proves it. People aren't products. They're not going to say what you want them to say. Real people have opinions you won't like.

Being real matters. A fake photo and profile might get you more views, but it isn't going to make someone like you in the long run. You might like a fake photo and profile, but at some point you're bound to find out who that person actually is.

Ben: "If a girl sounds too perfect, she's a guy."

Kyle: "There are a lot of dudes catfishing online. They know what we want, so they put up pictures of hot girls and pretend they really like us. Guys can get taken in."

Kayla: "It's hard not to catfish, because people don't talk to you if you're real. Most sites are completely saturated with catfish."

Shannon: "I just can't believe guys would buy it. How dumb are they?"

Ben: "We're pretty dumb. Most guys aren't as experienced as we want you to think we are."

The ability to predict what people want and like is a skill, but you can simulate it in your own life by asking yourself one question:

If I were my crush,
        would I want to be with me?

Here's what you're not going to do. You're not going to list all the fantastic traits about yourself as if you were your mom talking to your grandma about her wonderful child. You're not going to think up every negative trait about yourself and launch into a sadness that would make onions cry.

Just be honest about the kind of person someone else might want. Realize that you aren't that person. Nobody is that person.

We all have flaws, screw-ups, and really, truly undesirable traits. The difference between mere mortals and players must be that players are better at hiding those traits, yes? The answer might surprise you.

Kyle: "I have slept with a lot of girls, and I've never lied to any of them."

Shannon: "Nope. I let it all hang out there. I mean, okay, there's some stuff you have to hide. I don't want a guy to know if I wear bunny slippers or pick my nose in bed."

Kayla: "Yeah, but you don't put up some fake picture on a dating site."

Be as real as you can afford to be without oversharing. The first date is not the time to tell someone about your collection of waifu pillows or your bird skeleton mobile.

Also, remember that other users might lie to protect their own safety. You wouldn't mention that you have kids on a dating site, and neither would they.

lyin' and truthin'

DON'T TELL PEOPLE

-if you have a criminal record, unless it is directly related to your ability to date them.
-your personal habits, if they are disgusting (girls don't want to know how often you masturbate and to which porn)

-how much money you make.
-your address, before the third date
-your political viewpoint, or that of your family (unless you're dating an MPP you met at a liberal party rally, never talk politics)
-the nature of your racism, even if you think you're not that racist.
-anything sexist. If it begins with "all men" or "all women" just don't say it.
-how you feel about your ex
-how they compare to a celebrity you like, your ex, or anyone else in your life.
-how hot you think someone else is.
-how hot you think they are, more than three times in one conversation.
-that you're an international spy who drives a benz and saves lives daily. Unless you are an international spy who drives a benz and saves lives daily. In which case, please write your phone number here and return this book to the authors.

_____

Your name and number here.
(Please attach sexy photo)

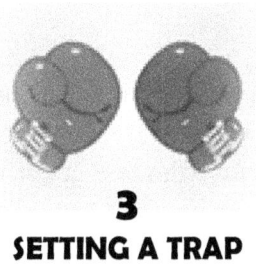

3
SETTING A TRAP

You know what you want. It's not the lop-eared street cat with the flea problem who you're pretty sure is only living on the street because he murdered his owners. It's not the fluffy purebred in the window who is going to pee all over your house the minute you walk through the door. If you even make it through the door first.

You need a cat who loves hiking, because you love hiking. Not a cat who SAYS he loves hiking, but can't walk two blocks without getting winded.

You haven't told your prospective kitten that YOU love hiking when you would really rather watch Netflix, so she isn't hyper and trying to jump out the door to leave you wishing you'd never met her.

Now What?

No matter how much you want Mr. or Ms. Right, waiting around with a realistic understanding of who you want, what traits they would have, and all that other chapter one and two nonsense, isn't going to keep your best friend from taking her home instead of you.

Kayla: "This is going to be the only chapter most guys want to read."

Kyle: "I should be writing it by myself."

Ben: "I don't even know why I'm here. How do I meet people? I just sit there."

Shannon: "You must not meet a lot of people."

Ben: "I only need to meet one."

Whether you're trying to meet one cat or a hundred cats, the same lures work. What do you do if you want to attract animals to your yard? Do you run after them with a huge group of friends and hope they run slower than you? No.

You plant catnip to entice them, put out food to reel them in, and leave the shed door open so they'll be drawn in by the warmth. Humans are mammals and like it or not, we work the same way.

Asking yourself what men or women want isn't going to give you an answer. Men and women want different things, not because they are born with a penis or a vagina, but because all of us live different lives.

Ben: "Sure, all women are different. But they usuallly all want the same guy."

Kyle: "Like I said, I should be writing this chapter."

Kayla: "Look at Kyle though. I'd date him, if he had kept his mouth shut."

Kyle: "Keep my mouth busy and.."

[commentary removed so that we could print this book without a perv warning]

If all guys want "the same" girl, and all girls want "the same" guy, then there must be some traits those people have in common. Here's what our players had to say about what draws our interest when we're thinking of dating someone.

personal hygiene

Whether you're going to the store or just grabbing the newspaper, it's important to remember that people (and potential dates) are everywhere. You don't need to pull out the expensive cologne or the $50 gold leaf makeup every time you go out to do your laundry, but please do:

brush your teeth and use chapstick

Kayla: "When I was in middle school, I used to walk out of the house every day thinking a boy might kiss me. I don't think I've ever really changed."

Kyle: "I can't stand being dirty. It's just gross to me. I can't imagine being with a woman who didn't take care of herself."

Ben: "I don't complain about makeup just because it looks fake. Mostly, I'm grossed out by how dirty it is. If a girl leaves stains on my white shirt, that's gross."

brush and style your hair

Ben: "To be honest, the first thing I notice about a girl is her hair. I notice it before her body, eyes, anything. If it's dirty, forget it."

Kyle: "I used to date this girl who always wore her hair in an adorable little ponytail. Oh my god. It was hot."

Shannon: "I think if a guy does his hair he looks better off, too? I'm thinking to myself, this guy can afford hair products and he knows how to use them. He's not sitting at home playing video games or watching TV."

shower and shave

Don't just shower and shave, but do it AGAIN before a date. Guys, get rid of that 5:00 shadow. Girls, give your legs the once over. Touch up your makeup. Even if you're just meeting someone for lunch, it has been four hours since you got ready this morning. Make an effort. Wouldn't you want them to make an effort for you?

Kyle: This is a dating book, it's not for kids. So I can give real advice, right?

Editor: It sounds like you're going to anyway.

Kyle: You don't have to print it, but...wash the D. I'm serious. Wash. The. D.

Shannon: Oh my God yes! There's nothing worse than you're about to go down on a guy and he reeks. It's disgusting. They think you're rejecting them because they're ugly or whatever and it's really that they smell.

the extras

Kayla: When I go out, I wear two bras. One underneath and a sports bra on top. It gives me so much cleavage. And I try to wear something that sparkles, because it's eye catching. Not like, a full sequin dress, but maybe a crop top with sequins under a sheer shirt. Guys go nuts when they think they can see your underwear, even if it's just a crop top or something. That's hot to them.

Shannon: Definitely. Bare shoulders, a strap hanging out. This one guy I dated explained it to me. If it looks like I can get you out of your clothes really fast, I'm going to hit on you.

Kayla: But not slutty.

Shannon: Yeah, not slutty. You don't want him to think you would have gone home with any guy. And if he says he likes girls without makeup, wear more foundation and less lipstick.

Kayla: Yeah. He pretty much means he wants you to be naturally perfect, which nobody is. Pretend you're not wearing it, but wear it.

Kyle: The girls were commenting that my nails look nice for a guy. I always get them done. Not with diamonds or beads or anything like that, but with just clear nail polish. You know, I don't want to hurt any girls.

Ben: Women go for my clothes, and my hair. There are probably more hair products in my bathroom than there are in hers.

Kyle: Go to the gym. Some guys could be really cut if they went a couple times a week.

Ben: I disagree with that shaving bit, too. I don't shave before a date. Not shaving can make you look more rugged. Like you just climbed a mountain then slid down into this restaurant. It's kinda hot.

Being attractive isn't necessarily about what you look like. From now on, take a second look at the people commanding attention when you walk into a room. Who is drawing the most glances? Why?

Our players, in between punches, wrote out a laundry list of things you should do when you walk into a crowded room full of people. It's how they get noticed, and it works!

5 ways to own the room like a pro

1. make eye contact with everyone
When you walk into a room, certain people and objects will draw your eye. Instead of dwelling on one person (or short dress), look everyone in the room in the eye. Players are successful because they don't limit their interactions. If someone returns your eye contact, talk to them.

Kayla: If a guy is standing there with four other guys staring at me, I think he's a douche. Put the same guy in front of a sixty year old woman who just lost her husband, and he's smiling at me? Guess who gets the girl?

2. be non-threatening
Remember Ben saying that he doesn't do anything to pick up girls? He might be doing more than he thinks. The goal here is to bait a trap, not run around chasing a mate. Staying still and doing something interesting is a great way to attract people: just look at how many phone numbers get tossed in buskers' guitar cases (a lot). Instead of working the party, try cooking something up in the kitchen, drawing a picture, or playing a song on the guitar. Ham it up!

3. help out

We're used to talking to clerks behind the counter at stores, EMT's, and other service professionals. What does this mean for you? An instant in with anyone you want to speak with. Instead of rolling into an event with five of your friends, consider volunteering there alone. If you're invited to a house party, offer to carry the food or collect empties.

4. make excuses to touch people

Tap a girl gently on the shoulder when you're pointing something out. "Accidentally" fall into a guy's lap. Hug everybody you meet. Use a caressing touch rather than the back-slap you would use with your friends. This lets the person know that you are available, interested, and (a bonus point) makes them think about what you might be like in bed.

5. don't over-commit

We can all read body language. Don't ignore it. If you're leaning toward someone who is leaning away from you, they're just not that into you. Even once you're on a date, it's important to read the signals and understand when someone is bored, tired, or just done. When the conversation lags, get their contact information and walk away. Make an excuse, head to the bathroom, but go. Fast.

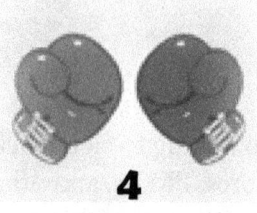

4

LET GO OF YOUR STUPID REASONS FOR LIKING PEOPLE

In chapter two, we talked about being honest with yourself about the kind of person you might get. It can be good to think of a relationship as a car loan, and ask yourself if you qualify.

The other side of that, though, is dating down. We do it for all kinds of reasons.

Kayla: I dated a guy for three months, slept with him once, and right after he started talking about his ex and criticizing my body. That kind of thing doesn't usually get to me, but this did. I really hated myself. I started turning down really attractive, nice guys who were interested in me and dating the biggest jerks. I dated one guy who was unemployed and hardly ever showered. What killed me was that he was so judgemental!

Ben: One of my friends dated a hooker. We thought he didn't know. We made a video of her taking money and getting into a car on the street corner, to show him.

the Thought Provoking case study where Shannon lost a friend and gained a perspective.

When I first moved here, I didn't really know anyone. I ended up talking to a girl at the dog park. We both had dogs. We both wanted to get more exercise. She was doing that marathon training program. Learn to Run, I think it's called.

We agreed to meet up and go running. I think we went a total of once. She gave up after three blocks because running was too hard. We ended up going for walks with the dogs instead.

I still ran, but she didn't.

Over time, I started to feel like she wasn't someone I wanted around. She was rude and often smelled terrible. I guess the bathing thing applies to friends as well as potential lovers.

Some of her opinions were just ridiculous. She allowed her daughter to hit other children because she believed that it would teach the kid how not to get raped in the future. In her opinion, it was teaching her daughter to fight back. I asked her what she would do if the kid kicked some poor little boy in the nuts. She was like, then he got what he deserved for touching her. I saw that kid kick, sratch, hit, and bite so many boys at the park, and she would yell at the parents. Congratulate her kid. It was so wrong.

She'd say racist things constantly, and blame it on her "crazy red neck" family....she had been raised by racists so she sometimes said racist things, in her words, "on accident."

I met her husband, and he was this quiet, nice, soft spoken guy. I couldn't figure out why he would be with her. He was always clean, and she was a slob. He smelled like cologne, and she smelled like the inside of a dumpster. He went to work for 16 hours a day and then went home to make dinner for his family.

When my boyfriend at the time talked to him, I finally got it. This guy had an idea in his head. He wanted to be nice to the kind of girl who couldn't normally meet anyone, someone who he'd feel charitable dating. He had been through hard times in his life, and wanted to save somebody who needed him. It had to be a white girl, of course.

Countless studies have proven that, their own race aside, most people swipe right on white. Thinner girls and more muscular guys are more likely to get hits and messages. Models are constantly fending off interest, while mortals can hardly get one person to speak to them.

There are preferences, and there are stupid reasons for disliking people. Liking people for stupid reasons isn't just bad for your dating life: it's bad for your entire life.

A few stupid reasons to like someone:

1. Mutual racism, or their adherence to your racist "preferences"

2. Having a jesus complex. Dating someone because you want to help or save them.

3. The way they look, regardless of anything else about them. Just because you're both at the same level of attractiveness doesn't mean you're compatible.

4. Their age. Don't date someone just because you're flattered that someone younger would want you, or because you think someone older can't leave you.

When we talk about liking someone for stupid reasons, we mean abusive, superficial, or co-dependant reasons. Liking someone because you can hurt them, or because they will help you to hurt someone else.

People get into these relationships all the time, and it's because we have lost the ability to understand the difference between our WANTS and our NEEDS.

As the Stones, in their great wisdom said: "You can't always get what you want, but if you try sometimes, you get what you need."

That applies to relationships, too. If you're trying to quit drinking, and you get into a relationship with a heavy drinker, it isn't going to work out in the long run. As much as your reptilian brain wants to drink, the part of you that wants to be a better person is going to keep rejecting your relationship.

What addictions do you suffer through, and what kind of person will enable them? When you're talking to and interacting with others, be sensitive to your own issues and on the lookout for the stupid reasons why you might date someone. You might even hear celebrities and social media praising this kind of relationship.

There are so many ways to date someone for stupid reasons, but a few stood out for us while talking about stupid, stupid choices.

I hate myself, so I deserve this person

Don't ever tell yourself that you deserve to be with someone who treats you poorly. We all know abusive relationships that are like this, but some relationships don't need hitting to be abusive.

Kayla: I used to know a guy who walked around with naked pictures of his girlfriend on his phone and showed them off all the time. She was way prettier than him, too. You could see that she wanted to say something about him 'showing off' like that, but she didn't. She just seemed so broken.

I'm ugly/fat. I can't do any better

There are people who will prey on your negative feelings about yourself, and our society can make it pretty easy for them to do this. There's never been an easier time to victimize people, because the internet puts all of us on display. We know how to push each other's buttons, because we know which buttons are being pushed every day all over social media.

Kyle: A lot of people think they deserve a better looking person than them, but that they deserve to be treated like crap by that person. It's weird.

I'm an addict. Only another addict will understand me.

If you have issues with drug or alcohol abuse, you might date other addicts, people who will help you to keep using. It's easier, when you're drinking or using drugs, to spend time with people who don't "harsh your mellow", but that's not the person you need right now. Someone who genuinely cares about you will discourage you from doing things that will mess you up.

I can change this person.

People don't change unless they want to. You can't force someone to make a change in their own life. No matter how much you yell, scream, cry, and beg, that person will still be the slob, drug addict, angry person, or alcoholic you met day one.

IS IT TOXIC?

It can be difficult to know if you're hanging out with someone who is toxic. Whether you're friends with someone, dating them, or just an FWB, steering clear of bad situations will help you to form better (for you) relationships. STAY AWAY if....

1. Everything they say is backhanded. "Don't worry, I'll make dinner. You just relax. I know it's SUPER HARD sitting at a desk and doing NOTHING all day."

2. They "forget" important events, details, or even your name.

3. They emotionally blackmail you. Every time you say you're going out to see a friend, this person wants you to spend time with them instead.

4. They alienate you from your friends and family. You invite them to a family party, and they surprise you with a dinner the same day for example.

5. Nothing you do is ever right. The way you talk is wrong. The way you think is wrong. The way you dress is totally wrong.

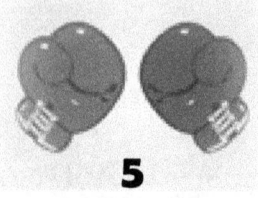

5

LET GO OF YOUR IDEAS ABOUT THE OPPOSITE SEX

Sometimes, even the experts make wrong assumptions about people based on gender. The things we truly believe about others without getting to know them first can hold us back in relationships.

have you ever said

"Girls only want guys who have money."

"Guys only care what I look like. They don't want me for who I am."

"Guys only want sex"

"A girl will date any guy, as long as he's rich or has a big D"

"Every woman is obsessed with kids and marriage."

"Women need to be drunk to sleep with you, so they have an excuse."

We're not always aware of our own weird ideas. Luckily, the people around us will be happy to point them out. Especially if our ideas are about them.

Ask yourself, where does this idea come from?

Shannon: I was talking to this guy online, and he told me that if he goes into certain areas of Buffalo, he knows for a fact he will be attacked for having white skin. I asked him what happened to him in Buffalo, and he said he'd never been there. I asked him if he saw something on the news, and he said no. He just had this idea that he couldn't come to my neighborhood being white without getting attacked. I was really offended. We didn't go out again.

Ben: A girl said that I've never had any problems in my life and everything has been easy for me because I'm a North American white male. I was a skinny kid. Growing up, everyone including my dad thought I was gay. My family disowned me. People beat me up on a daily basis. I felt like I couldn't talk to her about my life and what had happened to me. She was never someone I would have gotten close to. I sorta hated her after that.

Kyle: I use people's ideas about me against them. I'm good looking and on the short side, so they assume I'm a nice, unassuming guy. Girls will sleep with me without even thinking about it. They never even ask if I'm sleeping with anyone else.

Kayla: I assume things about guys a lot. I haven't been in a ton of relationships, so sometimes I forget this guy isn't my ex. He's somebody totally different.

Your idea about this person might come from movies, television, or what you were taught growing up. The one place it doesn't come from is the person you are making assumptions about.

At some point, most of us have been the target of wrong assumptions. It's a good idea to remember what people have said about you. Here's a great exercise that will help you to remember that other people have their own personalities, and that you can't make assumptions about them based on their membership in a group.

Take out your handy notebook, find a blank page between the doodles, and write down everything anyone has ever assumed about you. How did that feel? Awful, right?

The next time you catch yourself thinking about another person in a negative way beccause of their race, gender, religion, or Netflix queue, remember how it feels to be judged.

Your goal, if you want to get close to people, is to make them feel good about themselves. No matter how angry you are about your last relationship, how bad you feel about your screwups, or how ugly you think you are, start smiling.

People will smile with you.

The first half of this chapter couldn't have felt good. It was hard to get through, because it focused on the negative. Being a player in the dating scene is about focusing on the positive and making people smile.

A superficial "hello" or an assumptive "you're hot, let's date" isn't going to do it, but being able to truly connect with someone is a whole different thing. What makes them happy? What makes them tick?

Being able to make someone smile or even

laugh is a beautiful thing, and players have mastered it.

Kyle: It's even better if you can make a girl blush. Don't just say she's beautiful. That's too easy. You have to really look at her. If she's wearing a short dress, she must like her legs. Maybe she spent hours on her makeup. Be specific.

Kayla: Yeah, and don't lead with that.

Ben: You can go too far that way too, though. You're complimenting her so much that you seem like a desperate creeper. Like 'hey little girl, nice red hood'.

Kayla: There's a fine line.

Don't be superficial

Kayla: It doesn't matter what a girl looks like, she has friends. Girls stick together. If you're insulting my friend, I feel insulted, too. I'm going to leave with her, not with you.

Kyle: That works on guys. You can say they look hot and they'll go home with you. But that guy isn't going to call you again in the morning.

the Altruistic case study where Kyle talks to the wrong girl to get the right one.

I was in a bar full of mostly dudes when these two girls walked in. One of them looked really rough. There was scarring on her face, she was overweight, and she was drinking. A lot.

The other girl was tall, thin, and a total knockout. The kind of girl any guy would cry real tears over. She was wearing a short dress with long legs and a pair of very high heels. I mean, she was gorgeous.

It was karaoke night, and it was pretty clear this girl loved to sing. The guy running the karaoke made his move. When she went to sing the Rocky Horror Picture Show soundtrack, he helped her out by singing the guy parts. She was laughing, smiling, and having a great time. So was her friend. I sat back and watched.

There were three or four guys sitting at the table across from the girls, also having a great time. Most of them were pretty rough looking too and I thought they might have something in common with my future girl's friend. I figured when it came to her, it was going to be me or the karaoke host. So, me.

One of the rough looking guys got up and sang "I did it my way" by Sinatra. He actually did a really good job, and I could see Hottie smiling at him. This girl was really into singing, and you could tell that she loved his voice. I sat back. I was done. This 300 pound idiot had her on lock.

It turned out the round wasn't over, though. When he sat back down, he started collecting money from his friends. It turned out they'd bet him to sing the song. The rough looking girl said: "You did that on a bet?"

The guy answered; "Why don't you shut up?"
The hot girl said; "Hey! Why would you talk to my friend that way?"
Suddenly, he gets this sincere looking smile on his face and says, "I'm really sorry."

It was pretty clear that he was only capable of being nice to girls he wanted to screw. That was my in. I went and talked to the rough friend, calmed her down, and offered to drive them home. Guess who was making out with Hottie at the end of the night? Not the guy who insulted her friend.

People can be detail-oriented. If you find yourself rating others in your head, stop. If you find yourself rating others with your friends, stop twice as fast.

Your ten might be someone else's five, and vice versa. Telling people what to think can keep them from finding happiness.

Shannon: I went to school with a guy who was really good looking, but he was into big girls. His girlfriend must have been three hundred pounds, and he absolutely loved her. Every day, all day, the other guys were on his case about it. He ended up breaking up with her to get them to leave him alone. I was so sad for him.

Kayla: And he's the hot guy. They're basically just setting him up to steal all their girls.

Kyle: A lot of guys still do that. Just let your friends be happy.

Ben: That's the biggest player tip in here. Let other people be themselves. Don't make rules for somebody else's life because you're mad about your own.

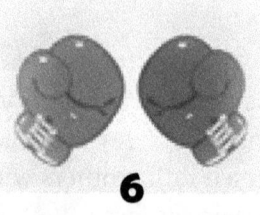

6
SPEAKING THE LANGUAGE

If we're all just regular human beings living on one big and inclusive planet, why in the name of creation can't we manage to talk to eachother without messing it up?

Maybe it's socialization. Maybe it's the way we're made, but men and women approach a conversation very differently. Our wrong ideas about what someone said to us can be the difference between "wine and dine" and "date and dash".

Shannon: I told a guy to go into my room and make himself comfortable. I came in with popcorn and my laptop, ready to watch some movies, and he was naked.

Kyle: Yup.

Ben: Women don't talk a lot in bed. They don't tell you what they want, or how to do it. Then you hear her complaining on the phone to her friends about how you messed it up. They think we're born with a vag map.

men strategize, women react

A common scenario occurs when two people are trying to make a date. Men see a first date or meeting as just another plan to be made. No emotions attached. They're going to get up, shave, go to work, come home, get dressed, and meet that girl from that app.

The plan goes on their mental calendar and is largely forgotten until they're about to show up. For women, it's very different.

Kayla: I want to meet this guy. We've talked on the phone, we've skyped, and I really like him. But he's pushing me to meet him. Like he keeps telling me let's meet here, at this time. I'm so freaked out by the time that time rolls around that I don't show up.

Shannon: I had a lot of guys say that if a girl doesn't want to meet up with them right away they just say forget it.

Kayla: What kind of girl wants to meet up after five minutes of conversation?

All: A hooker.

If you're not looking for hookers, read on.

What happens for the guy? He's met a girl he really likes online. She doesn't seem fake, and there are no filters on her pics (he thinks) Nobody's mining her pics to catfish guys.

Ben: There are a huge number of traps for guys online. Fake users are everywhere. Not a lot of real women use those apps, and it takes most guys a while to catch on. It can take months for us to get one message.

By the time a man has set up a meeting, he feels like he's already done a lot of work. The experience is very different for women.

Shannon: Women get at least 20 messages a day. If you're a hot, skinny girl with some beach photo you probably get thousands. The worrying starts for girls after we agree to meet a guy.

Kyle: I think it's the same online as in real life. Girls get hit on a lot.

Kayla: You have a better shot in real life. Girls get hit on less out in public.

Shannon: If I'm out, I already have my hot clothes on. I'm already having a good time. Online, I'm probably in my sweatpants.

Kayla: Posting pictures of that one time we looked hot.

Shannon: That one distant memory.

How can you plan a first meeting or date when you're dealing with the opposite sex? Realize that they don't communicate in the same way you do.

Our guy players said:

Don't decide how the date will go before you get there. Ask the girl what she would like to do, and if she says she doesn't know, don't panic. She's still interested in you, just a little freaked out by the whole getting to know you thing. Suggest a few places. If you can't think of anywhere to go, check out the first date suggestions in Chapter 9 or get to know her a little better by asking questions or stalking her pics to find her favorite hangouts.

Never assume things. Don't assume you've got this girl on lock and it's a done deal. The minute you assume that, it's over and you're not getting any. Just because you met her online, doesn't mean she's desperate. It doesn't even come close to meaning that. There are a lot of reasons she picked you.

Get competitive, not angry.

Shannon: I hate it when guys are like "are you talking to so many other guys you can't answer me?" Yeah, I probably am. But I'm making a date with you. So who cares who else wants me?

When they're at a bar, bookstore, or library, guys can accept that there is competition for a girl's affection. Online, the idea that she might be talking to other men can feel offensive. If she's messaging you, you are winning. If she's agreeing to go out with you, you are winning. If she forgets your name, just tell her what it is again. She'll remember it later when she's screaming it.

Hopefully not screaming "-Your name here- get the f'ck out!"

Our lady players said:

Being a people pleaser doesn't work with dating. Guys can tell when you're dating them out of pity or to avoid having to say no. Tell them the truth straight out, and don't make excuses. Remember, this guy just met you. He's not going to be heartbroken about you turning him down for a date, unless you string him along for months first.

Don't be an attention whore. Don't post your pictures online and message guys just to string them along. You're keeping them from finding a girl who might be interested in them. You deserve a relationship and so do they.

Get possessive, not competitive. Are you too busy looking at every other girl in the club to pay any attention to the guy you're with? So busy trying to get noticed by your friend's boyfriend that you can't get one of your own? We all have our down moments when we feel competitive with other girls, and f*ckboys play off of them really well. Bury them deep!

Kayla: My boyfriend would always stare at other girls when I was around. I felt so bad about myself until one day, I saw him out by himself. He didn't look at anyone and even showed the store clerk a picture of me on his phone.

Don't be a doormat. If he asks you where you want to go, tell him. Find an activity you both enjoy (there are some ideas in Chapter 9) and havea great time. Don't worry about him liking you: he already does!

men externalize, women internalize

Women think they suck, and men think you suck. We'll come back to this over and over in this book. Even before you start dating, this can already be an issue. Based on previous experience with the same type of behavior, you might come up with all kinds of ideas about yourself or the other person.

Here are some common ideas that can get in your way:

He didn't call (while he was at work) because he really doesn't like me.

I can't believe she didn't call me! She's clearly a flake!

He sounded irritated on the phone. Was it something I did wrong? Maybe I should just leave him alone. He'd probably be happier with someone else.

She sounded like she wanted to hang up. She's probably got another guy on the side. Some gym rat or something.

I don't need this drama in my life. I have enough to deal with.

RIP

here's another graveyard where you can lay
to rest all of your accusatory thoughts, if
you are a guy, and all of your self-punishing
thoughts, if you are a lady.

It's not her, it's you.

It's not you, it's him.

women support, men pump up

Men tend to think women are attached much sooner than they actually are, and one of the reasons is the way we deal with other people's problems. Women are socialized to be caretakers, and men are socialized to just get over things.

When a guy has the flu, his male friends will laugh, slap him on the back, and tell him to aim away from his shoes. Men are more likely to pump you up and say hey, you can do this, let's go!

Women are more likely to offer emotional support: bring a sick friend a bowl of soup or a warm blanket. Sometimes, a woman gets cut off before she even knows what's happening because her support is mistaken for love or even obsession.

Shannon: I don't want your address. I don't want your wallet or your cell phone. I just want to bring you some soup. Don't read too much into it. There's nothing else to read.

Kyle: It's the one time when there isn't.

translations from dick to chick

he says	it means
"I'm kinda busy"	"I'm having sex"
"Make yourself comfortable"	"I invite you to remove your clothes"
"We should hang"	"We should fuck"
"She's a slut"	"She's sleeping with every guy but me"
"Let's go dutch"	"I'm broke. Ish."
"I like bad girls"	"Please fuck me on the first date."
"I'm busy with work."	"I'm cheating."
"Ive met someone and I want to see where it goes."	"You're a crazy ass bitch and I'm out!"

we're talking peaches and eggplants here! peaches and eggplants!

translations from chick to dick

she says	it means
"I'm kinda busy"	"I'm kinda busy"
"Make yourself comfortable"	"Take off your shoes." "Unless your feet smell"
"We should hang"	"Let's just be friends."
"She's a slut"	"She's sleeping with the guy I like"
"Let's go dutch"	"If you like me, you'll offer to pay"
"I like bad boys."	"I think you're kinda boring."
"I'm busy with work."	"I'm bored. Make a more fun date offer."
"I've met someone and I want to see where it goes."	"I fucked someone because he got to me first and you are never seeing me again."

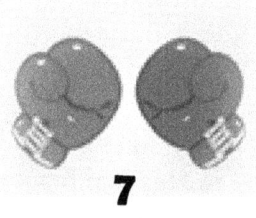

7

WHERE IS EVERYBODY?

You're single and ready to mingle. You go out to meet the opposite sex and they are....no where. Where are all of the girls in this bar? You cry. Where are all the guys at this Starbucks? You declare.

You're searching in guy places for girls, and in girl places for guys.

Shannon: There would be fifty, maybe a hundred guys in the club every Friday night, trying to meet a girl. But this place had been shut down twice for selling date rape drugs over the counter. No girls were going there.

Kyle: When they do go to clubs, they're literally GIRLS. Most of them are underaged and have no business being there.

Ben: It's not every bar though.

Kayla: Even so. You can't do anything with a girl who's drunk. She probably won't even remember your phone number.

Shannon: That's true. How many times did a guy try to give me his number, and I found it a week later in my pocket. But I didn't call

Kayla: Of course you didn't call.

Shannon: I didn't call, because I didn't remember the guy. I had no idea if he was cute.

This chapter is not going to tell you exactly where to go if you want to meet men or women.

But I came to this chapter for that exact information.

Yeah, we know. But back in the first few chapters we talked about finding the

right person for YOU, not for the person who sat down for eleven seconds to write whichever blog post, article, or other piece of mansplaining that led to you believing that ANY girl in the grocery store is ready to be

YOUR girl and any guy at the dog park is looking for you and your dog.

All that leads to is hanging around dog parks without a dog, and hanging around the grocery store when you don't need any food.

Ben: I met one of my girlfriends at the grocery store. It works. You ask them a question to make her feel helpful. Like, how do you tell if a melon is ripe? Something like that.

Kayla: Really? That happened to me a few times but I had no idea the guy was flirting with me. I thought he was just challenged.

Ben: No, they think it's cute. They want to help you.

The gloves stayed off on grocery stores, so we're going to call it a tie. Everybody needs to eat, so a trip to the grocery store gives you a pretty good chance of meeting a whole lot of people at once.

This book isn't about meeting a whole lot of people at once, though: it's about finding people who share your interests. Not just the right person, but the right person for YOU.

Wouldn't it be fun to make another three lists? Yes, we all love these lists by now. Grab a sheet of paper or three and write down everything you do in a day, everything you do when you have vacation days, and every last thing you want to do in the future.

You can even include things that you've had a lot of fun doing in the past. If you've time travelled, include everything you've done in the far past or distant future.

Also, please write of your adventures here, and mail this page to the publisher. It sounds like a great book:

_____

_____

_____

_____

_____

Awesome! Now, please ask yourself where the words "long walk on the beach", "hanging out at a coffee shop" and "watching a lovely sunset" come up on that list? Oh, no-where?

The problem with meeting people in the usual places is exactly that: they are the usual places.

Kyle: There was a beach where I used to live that had a reputation for being a topless beach. Every summer, you would see thousands of fat middle aged men hanging out there. If a woman had walked onto that beach she would have been mobbed. No girl in her right mind would go.

Shannon: Yup. That's the problem with telling guys where we are. They find out where we are and show up in a giant pack, so we stop going.

Kayla: It's the same for girls. How many guys are going to hit on me at a video game convention?

Certain spaces might have a lot of people in them, but because they are typically "male" or "female" spaces, the opposite sex is unwanted there.

Kyle: I'm sure you could meet a lot of girls at the spa, but going there makes you a creep.

Shannon: For sure. I can meet tons of guys at an MMA gym, but they won't be thinking "Hey, that girl who just tossed me on the floor! I want to date her!"

It's more difficult to find members of the opposite sex in this generation. Before the internet, there were spaces were guys and gals would mingle: roller skating rinks, dance halls, and bowling alleys, to name a few.

Our mating habits have changed, and maybe not for the better.

Ben: It's hard to trust someone you met online. If I haven't met her in person, I feel like she's already lying to me somehow.

Kayla: My sense of smell is really important in who I choose to date. Online dating cuts me off from three out of four of my senses. I have a picture and a bio.

Shannon: It can be good too, though. Going online is like walking down the street with some robot visor that tells you the age and singlehood of every person. You know all of this stuff about them and you didn't even have to try. It's awesome.

meeting people online

Online dating sites are great. They can connect you to people in or outside of your community, and even halfway across the world. People are meeting their spouses, flings, and fwb's on the internet, and the throng can't be wrong.

That said, the way we use online dating can be a problem. As we become increasingly alienated from other people, we start to use online dating as a substitute for interaction.

Shannon: One of my friends dated a guy for six years and she never even met him.

Ben: For me using a dating app is a step backward from meeting the person. I'm there to arrange for us to be in the same place at the same time, and things should progress the way they usually do from there.

Kyle: I'm not there to meet anyone long term, but it's the same for me. If she doesn't agree to meet me, I just move on.

Kayla. That's the problem for me. It's like a catalogue of girls, and I'm a product.

When meeting people online, it's important not to put too much value on the electronic portion of the relationship.

Ben: Meeting someone online is a means to an end. It's not the entire relationship.

Kayla: Exactly.

online dating dont's

DO NOT waste too much time talking to a person before you meet them. Someone who is very shy online can be outgoing in person, and vice versa. It's difficult to know anything about a person from words typed on a screen.

DON'T stalk, ask. So much information is available about people on social media that it's difficult NOT to look it up. Think of information posted online as public the way a conversation at a coffee shop is public: you might overhear it, but you are not the intended audience.

DON'T include a member of the opposite sex in your photo. The only picture you could find was from that work party 8 years ago? Take a new one!

the Informative case study where Shannon gets some shiny new stalkers

All of my friends were getting married to guys they met online, and I was in a single slump. I decided to create a profile online to see what would happen.

I downloaded the usual suspects: tinder, okc, whatever. I put up a profile and within a few hours, responses started to come in. Tons of them.

I think I had a hundred messages in the first couple of hours from tons of different guys. Since I'm a bit of a people pleaser, I tried to message all of them back.

I got a lot of this:

obvious don't...never ask a girl if she has a star wars vibrator.

even if she does... she'll lie. Because you opened with that

I thought that would be the worst of it, but it wasn't. Most of these guys had decided to stalk me in one way or another. It quickly freaked me out enough to delete my profile.

One of them found me on facebook and started messaging me there. I insisted that I wasn't the same person. Not because I'm a liar, but because I didn't want someone who I hadn't even met in person being able to quote details about me, my family, and what I had for lunch that day. Every time I posted, he messaged me some comment on what I was doing. It got really weird when he told me he'd gone to the restaurant I was eating at, but got too shy to go in. You say shy, I say stalker.

Another one told me that he was able to find out my home address by looking up the whois data on my website. A creepy person could have done something with that, and he'd be happy to help me fix the security on my computer. He included a screen shot with a picture of my house.

I moved, I deleted my profiles, and I only meet people in person now. I don't know how many of the girls on dating sites are real. I'm guessing not many.

meeting people in person

The reality is that whether you go through the process of finding someone online or wander down the grocery store aisles, you will eventually have to meet someone new in person.

No matter how hard you try, there's just no having sex with a computer screen.

If you HAVE managed to accomplish this herculean feat please, we beg of you, do NOT send a letter to the editors. We don't want to know how it was done. We saw "the video that shall not be named" already, and that was enough for us.

There's a detailed list of great places to take a first date in chapter 9, but it's not the only list in the world. The best place to go are the ones that make you happy, especially if you both like the same things.

If you love animals, volunteer at an animal shelter. If you're a great tennis player, join a tennis club. Do the things you love, and meet people who love them too. Conversation comes easily when you talk about something you really care about.

Q&A: How did you guys meet?

Random couples answer:

"On a dare. My friends dared me to kiss her."

"We were friends for three years, and then one day I finally just leaned over and kissed her right in the middle of a sentence."

"I decided to just say hello to every woman I saw. She said hi back."

"In high school. It took until college for me to publicly come out as gay. That's when he told me he'd always had a crush."

"The skate park. A lot of girls watched the guys skate but I got on the half pipe. He was impressed."

"I was volunteering with PETA and we started talking about animal rights. We talked for such a long time that we ended up going out for drinks."

"At a friend's wedding. I said we should drink every time somebody said 'cute'. It opened the door for a conversation. Before long we were talking and laughing like old friends."

how to talk to strangers

1. Use a buffer. Wait for your crush to be talking to someone else and put yourself into the conversation.

Kayla: I was volunteering with a charity, and an older woman started talking to me. A cute guy commented on what we were saying, and then asked the older woman who her friend was. I thought it was so cute.

2. Ask for help or advice. People love to feel needed, and asking for advice can start a conversation. Keep the conversation going by asking for advice about something that interests them. Walk up to someone on the beach and ask how he catches sweet air on his board. While looking at Travel Agency brochures, ask the girl beside you where she recommends going on vacation.

3. Show your sexual interest, but not too much. Countless relationships end before they begin because the other person simply does not know you're flirting. Make sure they know by dropping little hints. At the travel agency, say "Okay, but I'm only going if you'll be there." At the beach "I'm trying to learn but your abs are sooo distracting."

4. After you've been shooting the breeze for a few minutes, throw in a compliment. Tell men they look great, and be specific "That's an awesome tattoo, what is it of?" "I love guys with snakebite piercings" Tell women they ARE great, and be specific. "Wow! I never thought of it that way before!" "That's a great recipe! If I cooked it, would you try it?"

5. Meet as equals. If you're a dental assistant, the time to hit on a guy is not when he's sitting in your dental chair. If you're a TA, talk to girls who are NOT in your classes. When you are in a position of authority, some people will be more likely to say yes, but for all of the wrong reasons.

6. Smell good. As human beings, our sense of smell is fully developed in the womb and is the strongest sense throughout our lives. Our memories of smells last a long time. If you reek, that's all anyone remembers.

7. Talk to everyone. People respect authenticity, so don't be that guy who holds the door for a 19 year old model while a 67 year old grandmother struggles with her walker. For what? A head nod? Come on.

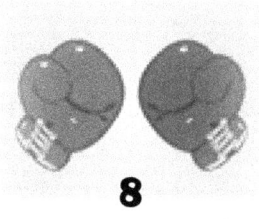

8

DOUCHESPOTTING

You've gone online or (gasp!) out in public on a fishing expedition, and found the one for you! Or at least, the one for tonight.

As long as you weren't too nervous to type nine numbers into your phone, you now have that person's contact information and the two of you are chatting about life, the universe, and everything.

The rest of this book might as well be blank paper for all of the letters to playboy and diary dishes you're going to be writing.

Why isn't it?

Because relationships are hard.

This chapter is devoted to weeding out the kind of person who you REALLY don't want to date. Before you even start dating them, follow our handy field guide to douchebags and maybe they'll learn a thing or two.

the wb (fwb without the f)

Kyle: There were a ton of scientific studies that found it was natural for guys to cheat.

Shannon: That makes no sense. Women can get off fifty times in the time it takes you to get it back up once. We're better at cheating, bottom line.

A wb is someone who isn't looking for any kind of relationship or commitment. They see relationships as a game. They chase the cat long enough to catch it, yank it's tail, make it miserable, and then throw it back.

Their favorite prey is the person who asks why, and loves to fix things.

Kyle: Girls were always asking me why I did things. That was my in. I'd make up some sob story.

Shannon, mockingly: I don't know why I'm like this. Maybe I didn't get enough love in my childhood. I don't know why they bought that.

Kyle: I guess I should feel bad, but they wouldn't fall for it if they got to know me.

The wb's weakness is *time*.

Kyle: You can't tell the difference between a guy like me and a guy like Ben on the first day. I'm going to tell you what you want to hear. So is he. But he's going to mean it. I'm not going to stick around long enough. If you say no, I'm going to try the hard sell and take off. We have sex once, and I'm history.

Shannon: Some girls want that, though. We're just not allowed to admit it. That's the problem. We have these standards of normal that force people to lie.

Kyle: What I don't understand is why some girls think you're in love with them after you have sex once. How is that your perfect world? I could be a drug dealing meth head and you're in love with me because what? I chose taking you home from the bar instead of an 80 year old biker?

Take your time to get to know someone, and wbs will dissolve. Because they are very good at manipulating people, most of them will wait less than a day before moving on to a new victim. Understanding some typical tactics can also help.

the wb's handbook

1. Get close to people, fast. Lean in and make them feel special. Take up a lot of their physical space. Make them feel there's nobody else in the world but them.

2. Show off your swag. Wear an expensive watch or expensive clothes. Drive a hot car, even if you only rented it for the weekend. Ladies, wear a short dress with your (only pair of)Louboutins.

3. Ask a lot of questions about them, give no information about yourself.

4. Somebody's always renovating your place. You need to go to their place. Better yet, you'll get a hotel. Leave before they get up.

5. "Negging". Give back handed compliments like "for a skinny girl, you look really good" or "I don't usually date broke guys but you're hot."

6. If the person says no to sex, get angry or offended. "Oh, you don't think I'm pretty enough?" "What, you don't date guys like me?" Make them think they're in control, when really, you're driving the bus.

the manipulator

You're not really sure how you ended up with this person, and you've been trying to get out of this relationship for a long time. It seems like they're never going to leave, and you really want to be done. Why couldn't you see what this person was like on the first day? It seems so obvious now.

Ben: I was dating this girl, and I told her we were breaking up. She just sat down on my couch like, "No." What was I supposed to do?

Kayla: My friend got home and his girlfriend and mom were sitting at the table picking out wedding dresses. That's how he found out he had proposed.

Manipulators are also looking for people pleasers: the kind of person who wants others to be happy. Their goal for you is a little different than the wb's, though.

Sure, a wb wants you miserable. A manipulator wants to take control of your life, forever if possible. While a wb might have no childhood issues, the manipulator almost certainly does. Like wbs, they can be male or female.

The manipulator's weaknesses are *friends, family members, public places, and logic.* If you are around other people, they will tell you how stupid the manipulator is being, and how much of your time is being wasted.

Their goal is to alienate you as quickly and efficiently as possible. At first, this person might seem like a dream come true. She's the girl who hops into bed with you on the first night. He's the guy who texts you at work just to tell you he's thinking of you.

Gradually, you start to feel like you're not seeing friends and family very much. There's always an excuse to stay home.

How can you spot them on day one?

Manipulators talk about their problems. A lot. You might think it's refreshing to meet someone so honest, but they're generally lying as much as anyone else.

Steer clear of someone who looks healthy but won't stop talking about a multitude of health problems. Often, their "problems" are undiagnosed, and it's the doctor's fault. Someone is always picking on them, and they need you to save them.

manipulator's handbook

1. Talk about how hard it is for you to get close to people. Pull away. Make them feel like the strong one in the relationship.

2. Ask for help all the time. Be helpless. Have trouble figuring stuff out.

3. When you do things, make sure you do them wrong. No matter how long you have been doing something, swear you never learned how to do it right.

4. Ask others to do everything for you.

5. Live in a messy house, and ignore any children you might have. Cry whenever someone suggests you should clean more or care for your children better.

6. Pretend you're sad to get out of doing things. Cry or yell to get what you want.

7. Accuse people of things you know they haven't done in order to get your way.

8. Blame others for anything that goes wrong, especially if they pointed it out, and always hear "yes" when someone says "no".

the narcissist

The narcissist wants everything his or her own way. Nothing you say or want matters. They are always right and won't let you get a word in edgewise.

Over time, you start to notice that your likes and interests are being ignored. You always seem to go where they want to go and do what they want to do. You feel more like a character in a book than a person, and the narcissist is the author.

Kayla: I once dated an actor. He wasn't really well known or anything, but people saw him and knew who he was. Whenever we went out, he was signing autographs and talking to random people. I broke up with him by just walking away while he was ignoring me. He didn't text me to find out where I was for an hour and a half.

Kyle: That girl who fixes her makeup in your sunglasses.

Ben: You definitely don't want to have kids with someone like this. My dad was never home because we didn't matter as much as him. He just did whatever he wanted.

The antidotes to the narcissist are *self love and the word no.* When you express yourself as a person, a narcissist isn't going to like it.

Kayla: He was talking on and on about his career and what he's been doing. I just started talking over him, telling him about my job and what's been going on with me. He excused himself and left.

Narcissists can't listen to conversations about other people very long. They love to boast about themselves, and always manage to turn the conversation back to themselves.

Their opinion is always right, and they may get into a heated argument with anyone who disagrees. They'll often express disagreeable opinions in order to find the type of person who will agree with anything.

Ben: If it wasn't about her, it didn't exist. Her eyes would go completely dead, I remember that. We'd go to karaoke and as long as she was on stage, she was happy. When other people were singing, she'd want to play pool or even leave. I remember this one day when someone at our table said the girl on stage was really pretty, she stomped off in a huff.

the narcissist's handbook

1. Steamroll every conversation with anecdotes about your own life.

2. Ignore other people when they talk, and walk away if the conversation hasn't been about you long enough.

3. Express your opinion on everything. If it's wrong, express it louder.

4. Form as many negative opinions as you can. The goal is to offend people, and date the ones who are too scared to act offended.

5. Look for loners, and people who don't get out a lot. You need someone who will cling to you.

6. Why get a parrot when you can date someone who parrots everything you say? Polly want a cracker?

7. You do everything right. If someone thinks you did it wrong, tell them to do it themself, or yell at them.

8. Do everything, and complain constantly.

The Professional

We all need money, but this person takes it too far. Work takes up most of their time. If they weren't at work too often even to see you, you'd think they were cheating. Steer clear of people who can't separate work from free time, unless you have a similarly busy schedule.

The Left Apron String

This person lives at home and pays minimal rent to mom and dad. Their sense of entitlement is only matched by their smell: when was the last time they showered? Who knows? Mom and dad do the laundry but they can't force a 30 year old to bathe.

The Yes Man

This person agrees with everything you say, no matter how ludicrous it is. Also, they agree with everything you do. If you say you'd like to base jump, they ask how high you want them to fly the plane. It might be nice to have your opinions validated for a while, but their parroting becomes hollow soon enough. You can recognize this person day one from the way they paraphrase you.

checklist for a good start

As Everlast taught us, "Where you end up usually depends on where you start". Here's what a good start looks like:

 You talk about mutual likes, interests and travel plans, not dislikes, rage quits, and health issues.

 They talk about things you'd like to try and places you'd like to go in the future. Their ideas inspire you.

 You don't feel an obligation to be around them, or like you owe them something.

 Nobody feels judged. You can show off to eachother and share ideas. Their smile makes you want to smile.

 This doesn't feel like a job interview. It feels more like a fun conversation with a good friend.

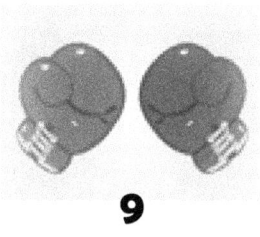

9

WOO-HOO! SWEATY PALMS AND AWKWARD GLANCES TIME!

Ah, those awkward glances, long silences, and stolen stares. What would a first date be without sweaty palms, dropped silverware, and awkwardness?

Fun. It would be fun.

This is one area where men and women can differ a lot. Women are socialized to watch the kind of romantic movies where a girl falls all over herself, makes a lot of mistakes and still gets the guy.

Men's movies are full of cool people with endless bravado and women who are happy with sexual relationships that have no other purpose.

Shannon: I think they're just trying to hire the same actresses though. They sell them to men by sexing them up, and to women by making them awkward. It's just marketing.

Ben: I don't think anyone finds an awkward date fun.

Kyle: I don't.

Kayla: I mean, there's awkward cute, and then there's awkward watching him stare at my boobs for thirty minutes.

Consider each new stage of your relationship a chance to make a new first impression, and act accordingly. Even if you met this person at the laundromat dressed in your Sunday worst, you have a chance to plan now.

This chapter is full of quick tips and tricks that will get you through your date without a hitch. Just ask the people who have dated our players:

Kayla: On our first date, he said nothing had ever gone as smoothly as it did with me. He really enjoyed spending time with me.

Ben: She thanked me for the date and asked me up to her apartment. I politely said no. She was all over me after that. Who knew "no" was an aphrodesiac?

Kyle: What can I say? I got laid.

where to go on a first date

People have different interests, but certain places work well for any first date.

1. THEME PARKS AND ATTRACTIONS.
There's nothing better than a ride to get you working together, holding hands, and having fun. The cotton candy doesn't hurt either.

2. MUSEUMS AND GALLERIES
Walking around the exhibits can gloss over any lulls in the conversation and give you something to talk about.

3. SPECIAL EVENTS
The town fair, the city's free outdoor art show, festivals, and other special events can be cheap or free while also feeling like an expensive night out. You're guaranteed to have a great time while supporting local artists and artisans.

4. LIVE SHOWS
If you must go to a restaurant or coffee shop, consider one with a live show, board games, or a secondary purpose. Play pool or darts. A little friendly competition never hurt anyone. Missing a shot in pool is the cute kind of awkward, unlike spilling coffee on your date.

don't know what to say?

1. Think about something funny that happened to you in the past. Smile, look your date partner in the eye and say "I'm sorry I zoned out. I was just remembering this funny thing that happened to me in college"...and proceed to tell the story.

2. Ask a question or make a comment about the decor. "Hey, the guy in that painting looks like me. Do you see the resemblance?"

3. Talk to someone else. Maybe the old couple celebrating their 30 year anniversary in the next booth, the waiter, or a little kid. Take the focus off the other person and they'll open up more easily.

4. Bring up something (light) that happened in the news, or make a reference to pop culture. Did you see that new movie that just came out? Did a dog save a baby from a well? Talk about it.

5. Bring a distraction.

Kayla: I always have a deck of cards in my purse, so I can offer them up if the conversation lags. It works great!

do not, under any circumstances

INTERROGATE THE PERSON.

The first date is not the time to ask for every minute detail of a person's life. Most of the worst dates our players went on involved the other person firing off questions one after another.

MAKE ACCUSATIONS

You may have had bad experiences in the past, but don't take them out on the person in front of you.

Kayla: On our first date, this guy said he was the kind of person who waits for both sides of the story before believing it. He kept saying that over and over. There was no second date. I still can't believe he called me a liar and acted like some kind of court judge over a tiny, irrelevant detail about my life. The sad part was that if he'd gotten to know me, he would have been in my life enough to know I was telling the truth.

ORDER UNUSUAL FOODS

You may be used to fried squid patties and

congealed blood pudding, but your date may not be. The first date is not the time to figure this out. Let your date order first, and then order something similar.

STARVE YOURSELF

You're out. Enjoy yourself. There's no reason to pick at a lettuce leaf for two hours and then go home and cry into your ice cream. You're not going to be any fatter or thinner in the eyes of someone who is already attracted to you because you chose to eat a human amount of food. Why is "I'll just have a salad" a cliche? Because it's really annoying.

EXPECT THE OTHER PERSON TO PAY

If the other person decides to pay for their own food/ticket or for both, sweet. Thank them and be super happy about it! However, do not expect the other person to pay. Don't take a timely trip to the bathroom when the bill is about to arrive, either.

DO DISGUSTING THINGS

This should go without saying, but pick your nose in the bathroom. Burp in the bathroom. Fart at home. I mean, come ON.

how to make things awkward

Maybe you never want to see this person again. Here's how you accomplish that.

1. Comment on the fact that they said everything they say. "You just said this place is nice." or "I don't know how this went from talking about ice cream to cats." No way! The conversation went from one topic to a totally different topic? Almost as if it were a whole conversation? Gee, whiz!

2. Comment on the awkwardness of the situation. "Wow, this is really awkward." It is NOW.

3. Speak positively of the people they hate. "My brother is such a dick, all he does is play video games!" "I love video games! It sounds like we'd get along!"

4. Be a creeper. You know how you coach your daughter's cheer team and have 200 photos of her doing the splits for some reason? Remember that trip to Belize where you took your son and his best friend with you? Wasn't it so funny when you all got drunk? You know what, this book isn't for you. You actually need mental help.

hung up on lies? here's the truth

"He/she is using the internet to cheat."

Dating isn't cheating...yet. A lot of people do go online to meet people and find dates when they're not happy in their current relationship. A lot of people also want to find a new house before they move out of the old one. Get to know someone before you sleep with them to avoid being "the other C"

"He/she is lying about where he/she lives."

The internet is a big, wide world of weird, and people exploit it to find out information about others. It can take months for someone to open up to you about where they live. There's a difference between lying and protecting yourself.

"He/she lied about having children."

If you're over 25 and you start dating someone, it's likely they're going to have children. It's a little weird to judge them for it. Most people do lie about having children online in order to protect the kids. This is only a dealbreaker if they're lying about kids they DON'T have. Someone trying to pass off a random child as their own is weird, and needs to be avoided.

"Ok, this person did not look like their profile picture."

Abs not as advertised? It happens. Good thing we've got a whole page on how to recognize a fake. Flip on.

how to spot a fake online

1. Too good to be true. If someone wouldn't look at you in person, they're probably not going to notice you online. Ask yourself, when was the last time someone similar to this person wanted my number?

2. Snapchat filters. Dog noses, fake flower headbands, faces zoomed in way too close (to hide the fake flower headband). Fake.

3. Similar profiles. When you're scrolling through the match feature, do you notice that a bunch of photos look like the same person? They probably are the same person: a model hired to keep you on the site, with her features and makeup changed slightly in each pic.

4. A blank profile or one containing very little information.

5. Stalk their instagram or twitter. 16,000 following, 800 followers, and 3 posts? Fake.

6. They ask you to meet up too soon.

7. They call YOU a fake. This is a common fraud tactic: making people feel like THEY are the issue.

dealing with bad dates

Tell the person the truth. You're both adults, and there's no need to keep them guessing if the date didnt go well. This doesn't mean you should make a laundry list of what went wrong and throw it in the person's face.

Hurtful as it seems, telling them the truth will benefit both of you in the long run. It allows you to give them a few pointers about what went wrong this time, so that their next date (with you or someone else) goes well.

Kayla: I told him that his arms were crossed the whole time. He was very closed off and it seemed like he didn't like me. I was genuinely shocked when he called the next day.

Ben: Guys are more sensitive than you think. I can come up with all kinds of reasons why you didn't want to go out with me again, and probably none of them are the right ones.

Shannon: Girls are the same way. I don't know what's wrong with me. The first thing I'll decide is that I'm not pretty. I could have completely offended the guy and I don't know it. If I don't know what happened, I can't fix it. I'm just left wondering what went wrong.

how much do looks matter?

When it comes to dating, some of us think nothing is more important than looks. We may not go out on a date or feel like it's going to end quickly because of our perceived inadequacies, and it would be really easy to sell this book by telling you there's some magic formula that will help you get "the girl" or the "the guy", despite your own looks/age.

We're not here to sell you attractive people.

Kayla: In high school, I was a model. I stood right beside a picture of myself and nobody even noticed me. It was very humbling.

People like to chase the cat they can't have. It could be some left over instinct or inherent trait but we love a challenge.

With this book, we're hoping to give you a more realistic idea not just of what can be done, but what you want in the first place.

Kyle: If I like to see movies, play video games, and watch tv, why would I want a girl who jetskis to work in the first place? She won't be happy, and neither will I. Maybe she's pretty but that won't make us compatible.

body language decoder

Body language can be confusing, but here are some of the main signals:

1. Smiling. If someone is smiling at you, they are probably having a good time. But watch their eyes: big round eyes with raised eyebrows can indicate an insincere smile.

2. Facing you. If the person is turned toward you, they like you. Especially when everyone else is facing in another direction.

3. Frown, knit brows. If someone is frowning at you, they were upset by something you said. Move on to a new topic.

4. Touching. When someone puts their hand on your thigh or taps you to make a point, it's an indication that they like you. Alternately, crossed arms, a closed posture, and leaning away from you indicate that they don't.

5. Wrinkled nose. Unless a skunk just walked by, if your date is making the "I smelled something" face, it's time to call it a night.

6. Talking about sex. If they're talking about it, they're probably thinking about it.

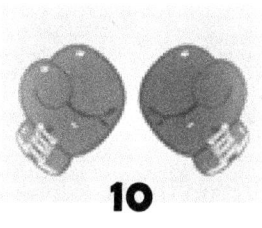

10

STUFF JUST GOT REAL

Hopefully, you can skip this chapter devoted to abuse. You've never been abused, nor have you met an abusive person.

If, however, you are healing from an abusive relationship, would like to know what abusive relationships look like on day one to avoid one, or have a child you'd like to arm with information, this chapter is for you.

From the outside, abusive relationships are very easy to spot. Have you ever said these things, or had them said to you?

"My friends say he's a jerk, but I love him."

"I can't leave her because she'll kill herself."

"He didn't mean to hurt me. He was just having a bad day."

"She said she was sorry and she'd never do it again. I believe her."

recognizing abuse

Abuse can start on the first day, or three years into the relationship. Certain forms of abuse are better recognized in our society, which makes it hard for victims of "atypical" abuse to come forward.

Men who are abused by their partners are much less likely to come forward, especially if they are gay. They are also much more likely to emulate the abuser in future. If we want to stop abuse as a society, we need to recognize that most abusers are people who felt victimized by abuse in the past.

They are repeating it to feel strong.

Female, male, or any other sexual identity, most of us don't know when we're being abused. Often, physical assault is the last link in a very long chain of behaviors. Physical assault might not even happen.

That said, people also argue and even get into physical altercations in otherwise normal, loving relationships. We can all have bad days, or be pushed to a point where we feel out of control, especially by someone who is close to us and knows our buttons.

am i being abused? am i abusive?

In the most dysfunctional relationships, it is difficult to tell the difference between the abused and the abuser. Fights break out on an almost daily basis, the neighbors hear screaming from several blocks away, and everyone knows you are "that couple".

Neither one of you wanted this for your relationship. You may even have had other relationships that were very successful. Why is this happening to you now?

Everyone is capable of violence. All of us.

Everyone is also capable of finding a solution to violence. The only way to truly stop domestic violence is for both parties to understand that no amount of yelling, screaming, hitting, threatening, or rage will make your issues the other person's fault.

your issues are your own.

Hitting is the easiest way to get someone to agree with us. We learn that as little children in the sandbox, smacking our peers with a toy and taking it from them. Some of us have never learned the strategies to stop getting what we want by using force.

how privilege contributes

It's unfortunate that some members of our society are less likely to be punished for committing assault. It's also unfortunate that when it comes to assault, it really depends who you're hitting.

While women are only slightly more likely to become victims of assault, our laws are lax when it comes to domestic abuse. When a rape is committed as part of an assault, it carries a lighter sentence than if you punch someone at a bar. If the victim is known to the perpetrator, assault is easier to get away with.

All of this sends a very clear message to the abuser: don't go out, get drunk, and beat up a random person. You'll end up in jail with no access to booze or people. Go out, get drunk, go home, and beat up your spouse.

Abuse is a pattern because the abuser knows they won't get away with it anywhere else.

abuse is not your fault. you can not prevent it, unless you are the abuser.

defining abuse

How can you tell an abusive relationship from a dysfunctional one? In an abusive relationship:

1. It's uneven. One person is always trying to please the other, who always seems to be on the verge of violence.

2. Violence is threatened by one partner against the other in order to manipulate that person.

3. Harm is intentional. One person strikes out, physically or verbally, with the intention of hurting the other.

4. There is no empathy. The abuser may also steal money, attack family members, threaten pets or children.

5. Abusers make insincere excuses. Their child "accidentally" felll down the stairs, their spouse is "so clumsy".

6. When they can no longer deny the abuse, abusers make excuses for themselves. They were off their meds, they weren't thinking straight, and they're sooo sorry.

the Frightening Case Study where Kayla placed an ad and got more than she bargained for

When I broke up with my last boyfriend, I decided to move back to the town where I grew up in order to make a fresh start. I was just feeling extremely lonely. I didn't want to try online dating in order to meet people. Instead, I placed an Ad on Craigslist.

This was my ad:

24 Year old woman seeks gym buddy. I'll probably go to Xgym but I haven't joined anywhere yet so if you go somewhere else let me know and I'll check out your gym. Female only please. I am NOT looking for a MAN, anyone to DATE, or anything like that, just someone to hit the gym with.

I got a few responses from women, but most were from men. Within a week, I had deleted my ad. One responder in particular actually scared me a lot.

He responded to my ad, first sending a photo of himself and saying he could help me train. Thinking he was a personal trainer, I responded and said that sounded great! I asked what his pricing was. He said he'd train me for free, and he'd also be happy to take me out on dates.

Uh-oh.

I responded that I wasn't looking for a guy at all, and he immediately started lying. He said that Craigslist had put my add on W4M and he hadn't been looking at W4W when he found it. He told me that I needed to stop eating what the doctor told me and start eating what he told me if I wanted to lose weight.

I immediately recognized someone who was trying to assert control over my entire life. He kept sending messages telling me how and what to eat, what to wear, and how to talk to people. After blocking his calls, I got this message in my e-mail inbox.

Wow ur still lookin? ...why would you say bye to me cuz I said ur being lied to? It's the truth! I know my shit! So stupid of u really...i was even gonna take u out for dinner and do things with you! So...good luck finding someone like me cuzz you aint gonna! Stop being stupid and text me back!

11 things abusive people do

1. Call you names.

2. Do something, and then immediately claim they didn't do it.

3. Lie so often you question yourself. Make you feel like you're going crazy.

4. Say something insulting, and then pretend they were joking.

5. Tell you how to think. Everyone else in your life is wrong and they are right.

6. Insult your friends and family members.

7. Isolate you while pretending to protect you. They don't like that friend of yours who is a major bad influence.

8. Treat you like a child who has messed up.

9. You're never allowed to say no.

10. Everything THEY do is YOUR fault.

11. Have a separate personality in public from the one you see, make you look crazy.

the healing process

If you have been abused in the past, it can be especially hard to start dating again. That's because of the way our memories work. Our instincts are stronger when it comes to bad memories than good ones. This helped our cave ancestors to avoid being harmed. When we touch a stove, we find out it's hot. As long as we remember it's hot, we'll never touch a stove again.

We'll teach our children never to touch stoves, and people will stop being injured by hot stoves over time.

What happens when our fear is of a person? Some of us will associate every person of that gender, height, or weight with the abuse. A smell, sound, or observation can put us off.

If you are on a healing journey, it's important to find out who you are before beginning to look for someone else. If the abusive relationship lasted a long time, you might be left with feelings of inadequacy, or an idea that you aren't really a person. Even though you might have been to therapy, there can be ongoing feelings of self blame.

At the same time, you are an adult with real sexual and social needs. You want to be close to someone, but it's hard with bad memories looming.

If you've read the stats, you also know that people who were abused as children are much more likely to become abusers or to end up in abusive relationships themselves. Healing is hard enough, without cold stats also making you feel like you're destined to be a bad person.

The truth is that you can heal from this, and that there are many wonderful and compassionate men and women out there who were victims of childhood and adult abuse. They have navigated the court system, been through therapy, and healed from some of the greatest trauma.

you can heal from abuse

As human beings, we are made to protect ourselves from harm. We are also made to survive. Being with others is part of survival. Being loved and cared for is something we need in our lives. On the facing page, we've collected a list of affirmations that can really help you to get healed and get out there!

affirmations for survivors

1. I know exactly who I am, and nobody is allowed to tell me that, not even a therapist, not even a doctor.

2. This is my body. It doesn't belong to any other person. Nobody has a right to touch me or even talk to me without my consent.

3. It's okay to talk about what happened to me. I don't need to hide my truth.

4. It's okay to say no. I don't have to be "yes" all the time. I don't have to please everyone.

5. It's okay to accept help. I don't always have to do for others. They can do for me as well.

6. It's okay to like myself. It's okay to think I look good, and strut my stuff. If somebody doesn't like me, that's their problem.

7. If somebody doesn't want to get to know me, that's their issue, not mine. I know how awesome I am.

8. Abuse does not define me. I am a great person with lots of hobbies and interests. Nobody gets to call me "the victim"

PART TWO

**RELATIONSHIPS:
HOW TO KEEP SOMEONE HAPPY AND SOMEHOW MANAGE NOT TO MURDER THEM.**

**I'M ANAL RETENTIVE. I'M A CONTROL FREAK. AND I'M A WORKAHOLIC. THAT'S WHY I'M NOT MARRIED. WHO COULD STAND ME?
-MADONNA**

**LAST NIGHT, YOU WERE UNHINGED! YOU WERE LIKE SOME DESPERATE, HOWLING DEMON. YOU FRIGHTENED ME! DO IT AGAIN!
-MORTICIA ADAMS**

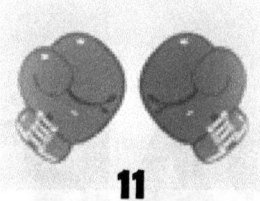

11
THE PERFECT RELATIONSHIP FOR <u>YOU</u>

Our players have changed but the game is the same: sitting in the comfy couch sectionof a coffee shop with some long-term couples, we researched how and why they're watching the meteors of other relationships crash to the ground while revelling in their own successes.

Maybe you stopped reading the first section of this book a month ago, and you're already ready to dive into a relationship with your new cat. Maybe you're dusting this book off 8 years later, finally ready to settle down after living the high single life for a happy, long time.

Whatever your reason for moving on to this section, congratulations! Our new players range in age from 23-75, with one very important thing in common: they are successful, happy couples with more than five years under their belts. The gloves came off more than once, but they agreed on some things.

the contenders

Heavyweight Class:
Janice and John are both 75 years old. They met in high school, and have been together ever since. This couple has been married for fifty-two years, and they're ready to give it to you straight with a one-two punch.
#relationshipgoals: We still snuggle on the couch, hold hands in the park, and play board games together.

Middleweight Class:
Emily and Will are in their fifties (and they're not telling us where!) They have been with eachother for twenty years, and have never gotten married.
#relationshipgoals: We work out together every day. Three kids later, we're still the hottest couple on the beach.

Lightweight Class:
At 23 and 25, Steph and Cameron come in at our youngest, but don't let their age fool you: these two met in their first year of high school and have been together for 10 years!
#relationshipgoals: We were friends first. We grew up in the same neighborhood and knew all of the same people. We made that work!

Will: I don't think we came into this thinking it was going to be a long term relationship. We just sort of looked at eachother one day and said, wow! It's been three years.

Steph: I agree. I didn't feel the time passing. I was just so in love with him that it passed by like nothing.

John: She was my first love. When I look into her eyes I still see the girl I met. I can't imagine being with anyone else.

Janice: And cataracts.

John: And cataracts. But mostly the girl I met.

don't look for long term

Often, we're asked what kind of relationship we want. The truth is that we may want one kind of relationship with one person, and a completely different kind of relationship with another. If the goal is long term, or casual, you could end up in the relationship you want, with someone you can't stand.

The goal is to find someone who you enjoy spending time with, so that time doesn't feel like it's going by at all.

Your ideas about marriage, children, and what kind of bedding looks best shouldn't be discussed at this early stage of a relationship.

Emily: We decided not to get married when we realized that many of our friends wanted a wedding, not a marriage. We wanted a partnership, not a dog and pony show.

set goals for yourself, not your partner

Relationships break down in the early stages when someone is focused too strongly on the relationship and not strongly enough on their own wants, needs, and goals.

The key to a happy, healthy relationship is knowing what you want for yourself, and finding someone who feels the same way. It's very different from treating dating like a shopping mall where you can decide which features you want, and pick up a brand! new! partner!

The beginning of a new relationship is a great time to explore both the things you have in common already, and the ones you have both always wanted to try. Relationships get stronger when you talk about future personal goals.

say this.......

"I've always wanted to travel to Venice."

"In College, I wanted to be an astronaut. Can you believe that?"

"I took dance lessons as a kid. I'd really like to get back into dancing. Would you come with me?"

"I like to go to the gym, but I have no-one to go with me. Do you want to go?"

....not that

"I don't think I could be with a girl if she gained weight after I started dating her."

"I really want a guy who is at least six feet tall."

"If I met someone better looking, I would probably leave you."

"You should go to the gym more often. "

"You're skinny, but you need more definition If I paid for your gym membership, would you actually go?

never manipulate a partner

Everyone tells little white lies at the start of a new relationship. We've all accepted that no woman was born with shimmering eyelids and bright red lips. Many a man who rented a Benz to impress the girl has shown up to every subsequent date in a Volvo.

Manipulation means lying about the big stuff to keep a partner trapped in the relationship, and it's not okay. All of our players have experienced this kind of manipulation, and NONE of them are still with the person who did it.

Will: I had a girlfriend lie to me about being pregnant. She wasn't able to provide a positive pregnancy test, ultrasound, or any other evidence. When I offerred to take her to the doctor, she faked a miscarriage.

John: A young lady came to our home and told my mother that we were planning to get married. They were planning the wedding when I got home.

Steph: He lost his job and came to us crying because hewas homeless. My parents moved him in. How could I leave him?

a guide to pregnancy and miscarriage

One of the most common (and worst) manipulations occurs when a woman claims to be pregnant with a baby who never comes. This can be deliberate, but can also be caused by misinformation. Since pregnancy can happen in any sexual relationship, this quick guide to the signs and symptoms of a normal pregnancy should help both partners to sort out the truth from the nonsense.

How Many Weeks? While early pregnancy tests are available, most tests are still not very accurate early on. A woman who is less than eight weeks pregnant can lose the pregnancy at any time. There is no reason to be upset about pregnancy loss at this very early stage. Thousands of women have miscarriages before the second month and mistake them for periods, because basically nothing is being expelled. This early, doctors don't even consider pregnancy loss a miscarriage and it is certainly not an indication of future inability to carry a child. This is not the time to break the news to a partner.

Blood Test is Best. A urine test does not confirm pregnancy. Go to the doctor for a blood test to confirm. There is no reason for a partner to attend the blood test. If it is positive, it's time to start thinking about next steps. Get a copy of the blood test result from the doctor. This is the best time to tell a partner about a pregnancy, unless you choose to wait for the first ultrasound.

First Ultrasound and Heartbeat. Whether or not a woman has chosen to have an abortion, the first ultrasound is done around the fourth month of pregnancy. Since most women are at least two months pregnant (because they have to miss at least one period and most couples don't time sex to be exactly the day a period is due) before they know about the pregnancy, most women do wait until this appointment to tell their partner that they are pregnant.

DNA Testing. Once a pregnancy is confirmed, DNA testing can be performed in utero between the 5th and 9th month. It can also be done after the baby is born. In a new relationship, it might be necessary to have DNA testing done in order to figure out who the father is, rule out any hereditary medical issues, and to find out if there will be health issues at birth. If a man believes the baby isn't his, he should expect to pay for the DNA test. and deal with the emotional consequences.

gold digger, dig that gold

There are many forms of manipulation in a relationship, but financial manipulation is one of the worst. Our players made a list of red lights that can warn you that a new partner is really just in it for the cash.

1. They are only interested in dating you once they see your stuff.

2. They talk a lot about their terrible situation and how broke they are, or outright ask you for help.

3. The person has a lot of stuff but doesn't have the kind of job that would support that lifestyle. If your new partner lives in a six bedroom house, wears designer clothes, and drives a BMW while sleeping until 3pm, you may have a gold digger (or trust fund kid)

4. Only calls you when they need something. This person never wants to go out with you just for fun, but it would be great if you picked them up at the mall to go visit some friends.

5. Sex is infrequent or nonexistent....but they'd feel like it if you bought them a gift.

give people the benefit of the doubt

If you've been manipulated in the past, you may find yourself always waiting for the other shoe to drop. Despite the very rare cases mentioned in the previous pages, most people you will date are genuinely looking for a real connection, and accusing them of lying can really turn them off. As a general rule, give people the benefit of the doubt, and don't accuse unless you're sure.

do this......

offer to attend the ultrasound appointment.

offer to meet the person at a venue.

tell the waiter to split the bill once in awhile.

e-mail job ads they might qualify for.

not that....

accuse her of lying about the pregnancy

get angry when the person asks for a ride.

become angry when the person talks about their money problems

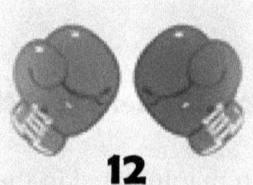

12
PEOPLE ARE STILL NOT PRODUCTS

Emily: I remember dating a guy in my twenties who broke up with me. He said I had "reached my expiration date". Good thing I kept him on social media. He might have had a good time back then, but this year he had his third heart attack. I can't imagine going through that alone. What he told me still sticks with me because we all have an expiration date.

Will: You keep me around so you have someone to drive you to the hospital?

Emily: I keep you around for more than that.

Will: Because you need a good reason to have a heart attack.

Emily: Exactly. Like your driving.

In Chapter 11, we talked a little bit about choosing a partner based on your own goals, not on their attributes. This chapter will focus in on who you are and what you need.

the three month rules

Steph: A girl I go to college with was going crazy showing off this gift she bought her boyfriend. It was for their three month anniversary.

Cameron: I'd think you were crazy. Three months is not a year.

Relationships run on pheremones until the third month. Our genetic need to procreate pushes us to have very good feelings about the person who chooses to have sex with us.

That's the science of it, but most of us could have figured out on our own that having sex with someone makes you like that person a whole lot.

Movies and advertisers are counting on this reaction when they show us half naked actors and actresses proudly displaying their sexuality.

Seeing someone who is attractive to us, kissing that person, putting our arms around them, and any kind of intimate contact can make us feel very good. When something feels good, it's natural to want to do it again.

Go ahead and keep on doing it, but don't get too close too quickly. The three month rules are fantastic guidelines that will save you from freaking someone out with a three month anniversary gift. Or six. Or nine.

it's not exclusive

You've been dating for a few weeks, and you're ready to get serious about this person. Great, but they may not feel the same way about you. In the first few months, it's common to treat relationships like dressing rooms, trying them on for a good fit. If you see the person out on a date with someone else, leave the issue alone. Bring it up on your next date and discuss it in an adult manner. Don't be exclusive, and don't expect exclusivity from the other person.

what do you know?

Knowing that you want to be with someone is not enough, especially during the first few months. As a general rule, it's probably not long term love if you don't know any important details like the person's favorite food or their birthday.

safe sex is great sex

Our players had no idea how early it's okay to have sex. Successful relationships can start with sex on the first day, or two years down the line...and so can unsuccessful ones.

With that in mind, try not to use sex as a yardstick for how well your relationship is going. Especially if it happens right after a breakup.

Will: I felt so bad for this woman. She thought we were back together just because we had sex again. I don't know why I said yes, because I definitely did NOT feel the same way.

In a long term relationship, sex can be really fantastic. Our players agreed that it gets better over time. The longer you know a person, the better they know your body. As long as sex isn't the only good thing about a relationship, it doesn't really matter when you start doing it.

You probably learned this in eighth grade health class, but it bears repeating: get tested for STD's before and after any new sexual relationship (so you know who to blame)

yeah...it was a lie

People lie to eachother in the first few months. At some point during this time, the person is probably going to come clean.

The clean slate can happen by accident (he says his mom is dead, and she looks pretty lively when she pulls up in her car to ask who you are) or on purpose (she admits that she wasn't really 27 when you met her).

Don't start questioning everything about the person. Just come clean about your own mess so that you can both decide whether this will work out.

i'm on probation

Don't take yourself too seriously during the first three months of a relationship. View this as a probation period at work. You're an intern. It might work out, it might not. At least you're trying.

we are borg

Spending too much time with someone can make them seem like a ball and chain. Keep up your own interests. Don't talk every day.

friends who?

What family? This applies throughout a relationship. You should never, under any circumstances, stop living your life because you met someone. That shiny new sex life probably seems fantastic. It IS fantastic! You saw fireworks and rainbows during your amazing lovemaking!

It is also only one aspect of your life. You know, the one you were also enjoying before this new person came along?

Friends who feel alienated by your new relationship might not be there for you when it breaks up.

Sure, you're going to be together FOREVER. But keep your friends, just in case.

love or lust

Numerous couples believe in love at first sight, and say they "just knew" that this would be their significant other on day one. What you're feeling in the first few months might actually be love, but you won't know that until later. If it is, you'll find out soon enough. In case it isn't, don't commit just yet.

the Horrifying case study where Emily found out the truth about her new boyfriend.

I was in my second year of University, and kicked out of the dorms because it was summer. Instead of going home separately, my friends and I decided to get a camper van and go on a trip to visit all of our families one at a time. Road Trip!

My friend Stacey rented a camper van, we packed up our stuff, and we were off. The first stop was my parents' place. They were really happy to see me. We stayed there for a month, in the front yard, and had a great time.

Stacey's family were expecting us when we got to her place. There were hugs all around, and they had this huge month-long itinerary planned so that we three girls could see all of Ottawa. They took us to the Rideau canal, parliament, and Cirque du Soleil. Stacey also took me out to her favorite coffee shop. There was always live music playing.

I met this amazing guy there. He had bright blue eyes and black hair like a Baldwin, played the guitar, and still managed to seem just really cute and approachable.

After a while I started blowing off my friends to hang out with him. He had so much energy and was really cool to be around. Unlike other guys I had met, he didn't talk over me.

We walked the canal together, went out for coffee and swimming, and he always held my hand. By the end of July, I was ready to blow off the girls completely and stay in Ottawa because I was in LOVE.

Stacey's family threw a party for us on the last day, and everyone was there. When my guy showed up at the door, I was so excited for the girls to finally meet him! I ran over to throw my arms around him and he got a horrified look on his face. Why was he blowing me off? We hadn't even had sex!

Stacey hugged the horrified young man and I got it. He was cheating on me.

That's when she said it.

"How do you know my baby cousin, Ems?"

Her baby cousin was sixteen.

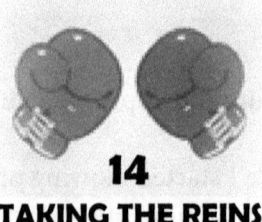

14
TAKING THE REINS

John: She did leave me once, for the longest six months of my life. It made us stronger when she came back. Before that, I didn't realize that things were so fragile.

Steph: You can get too comfortable with a person, and think they're never going to leave. If you don't take what they're saying seriously, that's a breakup for sure.

Will: I see a lot of relationships break up because someone is silently unhappy and counting the days, but the other person thinks "oh, he would be talking about it if something was wrong."

Live together long enough, spend enough time together, and you're going to end up arguing with eachother. Successful couples know that the right argument can make you stronger and the wrong one can break you up. Words can hurt, and they can cut twice as deeply when they come from a lover. An argument isn't about winning or losing: it's about moving forward from a problem.

In the same way cats will purr because they are sick, sad, or in pain, a person acting very happy in a relationship might actually be miserable.

The signs of someone faking happiness are easy to spot. If you are that person, it's more difficult to communicate your needs. Leaving the book open at this page might help!

how to tell your partner is miserable and hiding it.

1. This book is in front of you, left open to this page by your partner.

2. The lady doth protest too much, methinks. An unhappy partner will say they're happy. A LOT. Too much. When there is obviously nothing to be happy about.

3. Actions don't match their words. Slamming doors, practically breaking every chair they sit down in, and stomping out of the house swearing that everything is "just f'cking great!" No. No it is not.

4. Sleeping on the couch, or rolling away from you in bed. If someone is physically pulling away, that person is upset.

Miserable silences are a two way street, but the only person who can really break them is the silent partner. Sometimes, you need to take the reins in your relationship and let the other person know that things need to change. Preferably yesterday.

taking back your power

If this were a movie, the two of you would fall hopelessly in love and never argue, right? Wrong. That doesn't even happen in movies!

It's normal to disagree with your partner and it's even normal to get angry. Even really, really angry. Your big-kid pants wearing adult self can break down into a stomping, red in the face little kid, and looking in the mirror can become an embarassing prospect.

Arguments suck, and you want to do what it takes to end them quickly. Sometimes, that means agreeing to disagree, and ignoring the problem.

If you've ever had mice in the kitchen, ants in the bedroom, or vermin in the garbage cans, you know that ignoring a problem doesn't make it go away. You need to DO something about it.

better now than later

You may be afraid to tell someone how you feel when the relationship is new, but if something is really important to you, it's not a good idea to wait. It's natural to be afraid of losing someone, but they are probably just as worried about losing you.

Ask yourself: if this isn't a good time, what will be? In a few months when Valentine's Day rolls around? Next year when you're on vacation? If something is bothering you now, it will be driving you CRAZY by then.

assertive vs. aggressive

Have you ever held something in for so long that you can't hold it in anymore, and then started shouting and slamming doors? There is a wrong way to express your annoyance, and all of us have done it.

There is a huge difference between acting out aggressively and assertively telling someone what you need. We're very good at telling people how we feel, and it leads to a lot of circular conversations. "I'm upset." "So am I." Instead of telling someone how you feel and leaving it, try telling them what you need.

Try it right now by writing down something that is frustrating you at this time, or has bothered you in the past:

_____

_____

_____

If you have told your partner that it bothers you before, how did you say it?

_____

_____

_____

Did it work? Why or why not?

_____

_____

_____

_____

figure out what you need

Before talking to your partner again, you need to come to a much harder agreement with yourself: the difference between what you want and what you need. Don't take an all-or-nothing approach to the conversation, because you'll probably end up with nothing. Remember that your partner is a person, too, and there's probably a reason why they disagree with you.

Decide what you will accept before walking away. Anything you argue about can cause a breakup in the long run, so ask yourself, how far does my partner have to go before I'm out the door?

If you're arguing about children because you want six kids and a stay at home parent, but your partner wants no children and a house boat, maybe you can accept two kids and a canoe. Think about it before making your approach.

not the time or place

Never approach someone when they are stressed out, distracted, or tired. Don't start a conversation over text or the phone. Do it in person, or don't do it at all.

you're worth it

Don't let a fear of being dumped get in the way of a happy relationship in the long term. Remind yourself of everything you have done for this person before you start talking. You are valuable, and they will listen.

don't bring in a third party

Avoiding confrontation by bringing in a third party might seem easier, but your partner isn't going to see it that way. Asking someone to speak with the person for you, calling their mom, or telling the neighbor might work in the short term, but they'll end things in the long run.

start the conversation

Ask for what would make you the happiest. Use your partner's name. Keep physical contact with the person, to remind them that you love and support them. You are not the enemy, and a hand on the arm or resting lightly on their knee can remind them of that.

Keep distractions to a minimum. Make sure the TV isn't on, and no harsh lights are in anyone's face. This conversation is going to be very emotional, and you shouldn't be surrounded by ways to tune out or jarring sounds. Turn off the heavy metal for a sec.

Keep your concern to one sentence, and then let your partner talk. If you're not sure what to say, everybody loves a good madlib! Fill this one in:

(Partner's Name), I feel (feeling) when/when you (action word)(person) because (explanation) and I really need you to (action).

If you need a good laugh, you can always fill it in with your partner.

Michael, I feel desolation when you kick my cousin's gardener because my cousin's gardener is really a vampire, and I really need you to suckle.

It does, however, work better when you use your actual issue. John, I feel upset when you say that you don't want children, because I'm a teacher and I really love kids. I really need you to consider the posibility of our having children.

Whatever works, really.

two ears, one mouth

A conversation shouldn't be about waiting for the chance to talk again. Listen to the other person, REALLY listen, and try to see the situation from their perspective. They might have a good reason why now isn't the right time to move in together, buy a new house, or have children.

make sure something happens

Be calm, but firm. Do not walk away without a solution. If the other person decides to walk away, let them go. Stay right where you are until they either agree with you or agree to another solution that works for both of you. If you find yourself agreeing to avoid feeling stressed, or out of fear of losing them, stop. If this is something you really need to be happy, don't give up.

avoid emotional blackmail

Make sure that you talk about authentic feelings. Don't tell the person you are more upset than you are, and never say you're willing to walk away from the relationship if you don't mean it.

never make empty threats or empty promises

If you say you're going to do something, do it. Don't throw anything out there if you don't mean it. Always be prepared for the other person to say "okay" and make sure they're not calling your bluff when that happens.

get the respect you deserve

If someone ignores you, refuses to listen, or acts like your needs aren't important, let them walk away. There's no point.

regroup

After talking to the person, ask yourself what the conversation accomplished, and make a plan for what to do next.

know when it's over

If this is the hundredth time you've had this conversation and no solution can be reached, it's time to end it. End the conversation, or, if the conversation is extremely important and you're going to bring it up again, it could be time to end the relationship.

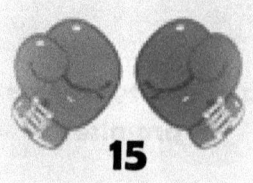

15

YOU SAY HE'S JUST A FRIEND

Our players agreed that every good relationship comes from a good friendship, but are reelationships really just friendships with sex attached? If they were, everything about them would be a lot easier, and friends wouldn't tend to be caught in the crosshairs of our spats, quarrels, and sexual tensions.

Since friends are so often left on the back burner, thrown into the middle, or hung out to dry with unrecoited feelings, we've dedicated a chapter to their longsuffering ways.

Janice: Things were different back then. These days, people judge eachother for getting married or having kids. Back then, it didn't change anything. That was still your friend. You'd go over and help out with their new baby, not call them from the club to laugh at them.

Steph: I don't want to say it's a generational thing, but I think that yeah, my friends have to be in the same situation as me. Single people don't want to hang out with the two of us because they're still looking for someone to be with. Married people don't want to hang out with us because they're working on kids.

Will: It's either/or half the time. People work so many hours that you have maybe three hours once you get home. I have to decide if I'm going to spend it with her and my family, or out with my friends.

Cameron: You see your friends on social media, and you think that's good enough.

in the zone...the friend zone

The media haven't deliberately done us an injustice, but in the case of love, it can be important to remember that movies and television are selling fantasies to us. It's about seeing the things we wish would happen play out on a screen.

Unfortunately, men in particular are sold an idea that women are sexually attracted (somehow) to objects, and not people. Men are led to believe that if they make enough money, buy enough stuff, or are nice enough to a woman, she will eventually decide to date them. This has led to the mythology of "being stuck in the friend zone." When a person, male or female, is "stuck in the friend zone", what they really are is stuck in a fantasy. They are stuck in the idea that the other person is, in fact, a friend.

recognizing a good friendship

Many of us have an idea of what a good friendship looks like: two or more people having a good time together, supporting one another, and sharing the same interests.

Friendships can be toxic and uneven throughout our lives, and "friend zone" friendships are arguably the worst ones. These friendships are uneven, and they are not about having a friend at all.

They are about the fantasy that this person who you perceive to be more attractive will one day decide that you are sexually attractive. People wait years in these holding patterns for the chance to finally date "that guy" or "that girl", putting their own lives aside to do so.

The facing page is full of harsh reality that will help with understanding the difference between real and manipulative friendships.

is this actually a friend?

A real friend.....

wants to hang out with you

spends time with you in public

doesn't ask you for rides, money, or to pay for anything.

helps you out and listens to you.

A manipulator....

only hangs out with you when somebody else breaks up with them or nobody else is available.

always wants to hang out at your place or theirs so nobody knows you're friends

asks you to pay for everything.

occasionally defends you (if they feel bad about using you)

hangs up as soon as you start talking about yourself

Cameron: I'm going to feel like a dick, but guys end up un the friend zone by having a completely unrealistic idea of the kind of girl they're going to get.

Steph: Or the kind of girl they even want. Nobody wants to be used. And I mean, they could be happy. Usually they know tons of girls that would date them, but they're holding out for some supermodel.

Cameron: It's sad because they could be happy but they don't want happy. It's like they're punishing themselves.

good friends can be total dicks, but that doesn't mean you have to dump them.

Your friends have been with you the longest, and they know you better than any new relationship. They feel safe and comfortable in knowing who you are and what makes you happy. They also have an outside perspective on your relationship, as people who are not currently making out or having sex with your partner.

Good friends are going to tell you the truth, and sometimes, the truth hurts. Instead of dumping a friend, consider asking them why they feel that way, setting up an appointment for them to get to know your partner, or using the pointers in chapter 14 to come to some kind of agreement.

Keep in mind that there is a big difference between helpful and destructive friendships. Listen to friends who genuinely care about your well-being and give good advice. Ignore the "advice" of friends who screw up your life, no matter how compelling they may seem.

jesse's girl

Love triangles have been around since Archie couldn't make a decision between Betty and Veronica: in other words, forever. For young people, they are a normal part of growing up and not being ready for an adult sexual relationship just yet.

It's hard to find the guilty party in a love triangle (or quadrangle). Go to any bar or club on a weekend and you'll see groups of guys out with one girl.

Do none of them have girlfriends? Have none of them dated in years? Nope. They're just waiting around for "the girl".

Many situations end up this way (one guy in a crowd of girls, one girl in a crowd of guys) and almost nobody has a good time in them. Let's define some of the usual suspects, and how to take them down.

the alpha douche

The alpha has a lot of friends, and tells all of them what to do. When it comes to people having a relationship, there can only be one: the alpha. Their partner is always better than yours, and they can't see why you would ever want to bring the mediocre humans you can attract out in public.

How to fight the Alpha Douche: The Deep Freeze. Get together without the alpha, and explain that your partners are uncomfortable with being insulted, or asking why you go out all the time but only the A.D. brings a date. They can show up, or sit home alone with their partner. Fine with you. Did you really want to see another makeout session while trying to eat your nachos?

the friend zoner

This person has a lot of exes, and a lot of people who really want the chance to date them. They're really good at throwing single gender parties where they are the guest of honor. Everybody's in the friend zone, and the friend zone is huge.

How to fight the Friend Zoner: Expand the Zone. When you're invited out, bring as many friends as you can, male and female. They won't mind, right? After all, they keep inviting a bunch of extra friends on what you thought was going to be a date.

the obsessive

Sometimes, you just want to hang out with your own gender, and this person won't let you. They're afraid that their partner is going to cheat wherever he or she goes, and even if you're going to the strip club, this person is tagging along. Their goal is to get you to stop inviting their partner out, so that your friend can spend the rest of his or her life on a choke chain. Sometimes, you think you should just give up.

How to fight the obsessive: The Carve. Carve out some space for yourself and your friends. Tell obsessive dates that you're not going out with them tonight, period. You're happy to send snaps, but they're not coming.

what the hell did I do last night?

DO NOT EVER SLEEP WITH YOUR PARTNER'S FRIENDS. Without their consent, at least. See part three for pointers on how and when it IS a good idea.

It's tempting. Your partner is this great person, fantastic, and fun to be around. Once you start hanging around them, you realize how many people there are in your partner's life: people just like them!

It's like walking into a buffet restaurant full of your favorite foods. What are you supposed to do?

Nothing. It's important to realize that your partner's friends (and hot relatives) are attractive because they remind you of your partner, but in a mysterious, haven't seen them naked yet kind of way.

If you really care about your partner, realize that by cheating with their friends or family members you are not only betraying a trust, you are taking away a support system. They'll have no one to talk to about what happened, and it will be harder to heal.

so this is my friiiieeeend

When should you introduce your friends to your partner? As soon as possible. As Chris Rock said; "If you've been dating a guy for four months, and you have not met any of his friends, you are not his girlfriend."

Most people are aware that a relationship that goes on too long without you meeting any of their friends or relatives is not a real one. They might start to feel like you're cheating or ashamed to go out in public with them.

Romantic relationships that are disconnected from your other relationships end early and often. Being on the receiving end of this can feel depressing and painful. If you're wondering why you haven't met your partner's friends or family members yet, it may be time to ask where, exactly, they think this relationship is going.

If you're interested in long term and they're just waiting around for a better offer, it's best to find out as soon as possible. None of us are getting younger, and nobody has time to waste on being unhappy or rejected.

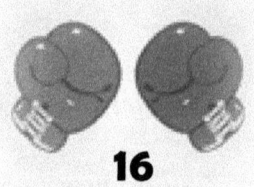

16

YOU WILL NEVER DATE YOURSELF

Ah, expectations. Nothing screws things up faster than the idea that everyone in your life must be exactly like you. Have you ever heard these heart-breaking cries?

"I have a good job, a car, and I work 16 hours a day. I have never had children. Is it too much to expect that the person I date won't have children, either? I mean, I'm only fifty."

"I work out every day, and I'm in great shape. I can't see dating anyone with more body fat than me. Why should I settle?"

"I didn't leave my wife and kids just to date someone who has children."

"I can eat anything I want, and I'm still skinny. Why can't I meet someone like that? Is that too much to ask for?"

Yes, it's too much to ask for. Not only of the other person, but of yourself. Having extremely high expectations of the type of person you will date is a way to set yourself up for failure. It's time to ask yourself the hard question:

am i doing this because i really don't want a relationship right now?

You might not want a relationship because it feels like your freedom will be taken away. Maybe you're not feeling attractive or special enough to deserve a relationship at this time. Or you just got out of a terrible relationship, and aren't really ready for another.

When our sexual thoughts dont match our logical and self-preservation instincts, it's usually time to make excuses. She was too short, he wore green: who does that; she had a dog, he had a weird left toe.

Are you judging others because of your own feelings of inadequacy?

Will: I was kind of a nerd in high school. I had trouble meeting girls. So I just threw myself into my school work and that was how I made myself feel better. They could get boyfriends and have babies but at least I had a great job. So when I was older, and some of these women were single moms, I wanted to hurt them back. It was all me.

be honest

Having an overblown sense of self-assurance is great when you're making sales, closing deals, and getting good grades in school. That might be why so many of us develop huge amounts of boisterous self love…as a coping skill, and a way of getting what we want. Aim high, all of the experts tell us, and you'll get everything you ever wanted!

Oddly, our execution when it comes to jobs is much better than our relationship strategies. We compared the things people say about relationships to situations in the job world, with hilarious results.

"I really want a job, but I don't like the idea of applying. I get really nervous when I try to apply for a job. All the work of putting in applications just seems like too much."

"Job interviews are impossible. I'm socially awkward at job interviews. I feel like I don't know this person very well, and they're probably not going to like me."

"I don't want to apply for more than one job. There's one job I want, and I don't care who has it. I'm going to go to that company every single day, early. If I sit in a chair long enough, they'll have to hire me."

Everyone knows that you can't get a job without applying, yet we assume that people will psychically know when we're interested in them.

We know that job interviews are awkward because we've just met the person, but don't seem to understand that dates aren't going to go smoothly the first time.

We become obsessed with one person or type of person, without understanding that there are literally billions of people on earth.

It's important to be honest, with yourself and with the people around you. People are not commodities,they are actual human beings who have experienced life differently from you.

If you're feeling insecure, finding someone exactly like you won't even be good enough. Someone just like you will have all of the traits you can't stand in yourself. If you don't like yourself, every similarity between you and another person becomes a flaw. Their flaw, because you can't leave yourself.

negative self-talk

Judgemental people can seem like the most confident people out there. They always have something to say about the way you look and what you're doing with your life. The focus is always on you, and you spend so much time trying to fix yourself that you may not notice the judgemental person at all.

Imagine yourself in that person's shoes. Imagine wanting so badly to be invisible that you pick at others with constant negative commentary. You'd have to be pretty afraid that people might find out the truth about you, or the way you feel about yourself.

The truth is that looks don't dictate the way you feel about yourself. If we were born alone in the forest, none of us would know or care what we look like. Our opinions of ourselves are formed by others, and those little seeds of negativity can get themselves stuck inside our brains.

I'm an eraser, you're glue

People insult you because they want you to fight back. They know that certain people are put in a privileged position over you (me, them, and all of us). When you don't respond to their insults, it gives them permission to love themselves. How does this work?

Emily: When I was in high school, this kid made fun of me for having a big nose. I felt like running home and crying. Instead, for the first time ever, I looked him right in the eye. I stuck out my chin and I went "Yeah? Well you have a big nose, too." It was this huge moment for me. Finally I stood up for myself and turned the lens back on him. He said, "yeah, I do. We should hang out." It felt weirdly magical to break through all that.

We have this idea that people make fun of us because we're fat, ugly, useless, pathetic...they don't. They make fun of us because THEY feel fat, ugly, useless, and pathetic. They need someone who they see a little bit of themself in to stand up and say, "who cares?" It gives them the courage to do the same.

Guess what? You're not perfect. Maybe you've been called names. Maybe you've been made fun of. Maybe you wake up every morning thinking "damn, I'm ugly!"

Don't be afraid! We've all got hangups. Just get out there and do you!

my partner must suck syndrome

Grandma always said you have to love YOU before you can love anyone else and guess what? She was right.

If you go into a relationship with a negative self-image, you're going to be miserable. If you suck, anything you date must also suck by association. No matter how amazing your partner is when he or she doesn't want you, that person instantly becomes garbage the second you start dating.

Cameron: My neighbor was constantly going on about his "hot, younger" wife. She was outside constantly washing their car in a bikini. He would even insult Steph, stuff like "I don't know how an old man like me got a younger, hotter chick than your girlfriend." One day I told him she wasn't that hot. He was so pissed off. He started working extra long hours and giving her dirty looks all the time.

Steph: Like she could never be good enough because he wasn't.

Your partner is not there to validate you or improve your status. Love yourself first.

let it go, let it goooooo!

It's time for another graveyard! Let's bury that negative self talk about yourself and your partner, once and for all time!

(Yup, that's what once and for all used to be)

rip haters

Goodbye douche move

Hello new you!

17
EXES AND OHS

This chapter should really be titled "How to get your exes the hell out of your life and live hapilly ever after." Our players, and every successful relationship they knew of, had one thing in common: no ex boyfriend or girlfriend drama.

Janice: The expectation when I was young was that people would stay together forever. When my sister got divorced, it was quite ugly. Everyone took one side or the other. Our family was split in half and forced to choose between them.

Will: I certainly don't hang around any of my exes. She gets upset when they try to add me to facebook.

Emily: Because they usually send you some beach shot of the two of you making out along with the message "hey Will, do you remember this day?"

Will: I was quite the adventurer when I was a kid. I don't remember any of those days.

things to do BEFORE you commit to a new relationship

1. Remove compromising photos of yourself from social media.

2. Un-tag yourself from photos of your ex, photos containing your ex, photos that were taken of your ex by you....if it belongs to your ex, and you are tagged in it, remove the tag.

3. Dump your hard drive onto an external hard drive or, if necessary, a NSA-protected server. Lock it up. Waaay up.

4. Get rid of all your exes clothes, chachkis, and physical pictures. Nothing lands you in the doghouse faster than a new lover finding the old one's underwear in your bed.

5. Get rid of any mutual sex toys, even... ESPECIALLY if it was a toy your ex really liked. A new lover will NOT appreciate you treating them like they are someone else. Learn what they like.

6. Get rid of any keepsakes from trips you both went on, engagement rings, or pictures you drew of your future babies.

the Sad case study where Cameron learns that you just can't be friends with your ex

A few years ago, my brother started dating this really nice girl. I guess he didn't think she was as status as his ex. Every guy we knew had a thing for his ex for some reason, and they were always talking about her.

This other girl was taller and bigger, and a bit older than him. They didn't know any of the same people. That's probably what screwed them over.

Anyway he broke up with his ex about a year, year and a half before he started dating the new girl. He was totally broken up over it. Literally wouldn't leave his room, because we all hung out with the same people and I mean, this girl was always around or being talked about.

He didn't get over her, but when he met this new girl he decided to move on. She was really nice and I guess he wanted to be with somebody.

At first, we thought she was his imaginary friend. He was out all the time but we never met the person he was hanging around with. When we finally did meet her, he was already pretty serious about this girl. He was talking about them getting a place together.

Fast forward a few months and his ex found out about his new relationship. She saw the pictures of him smiling and happy on the interwebs. The first thing she wanted to do was destroy him.

She sent him a message saying she missed him, and my brother was like "It's okay. We're just talking."

Then she started asking him to hang out. Alone. Super innocent, right? She said she hadn't realized how much she missed him until he found somebody else. Of course, they couldn't hang out together.

His new girlfriend noticed how often he was going out to hang out with friends alone, and felt like he was ashamed of her. They started fighting all the time, and eventually he cheated on her with his ex. Of course.

I just thought, what a couple of idiots. They were both cheating on somebody else with eachother. I swear they got off on it.

the camel in the tent
a parable, told by John

As a young man, I travelled the globe, and at one point I visited India. They have a parable there that is both practical and useful for real life. That's exactly what the man in the market said to me. He said, "Listen, I'm an old man, and I have a parable. It's practical, if you are ever in a tent in the desert. It will also teach you an important thing about life. Will you listen?"

Of course, I said yes. He sat me down and told me this story about a camel in a tent. He's right. This damned camel kept my marriage together a number of times.

The Camel in the Tent

When you are camping out in the desert, you must always be aware of your surroundings. This is because occasionally the desert will become cold, or lonely. That is when camels wandering across the sand will stop.

A camel lying in the sand is not very dangerous, unless there is a storm or it's dark, or he's separated from his herd. When a camel has a not very good day, he might see your tent, or the glow in there, and think "My goodness, this looks like a very good tent. It's sturdy and warm. I'll just stick my nose in."

When the camel sticks his nose in, you might think "What's the harm? It's only a camel's nose. What can it do? Nothing."

But if you let the nose in, be assured that the camel will then stick in his long, long neck. And even if you think to yourself, "Oh, what does it matter? That's only a camel's head and his neck. It takes up no space at all!" you should seize the camel and push his head out.

If you don't, he will put one leg into your tent. You might think "Oh, what does it matter? That's only one leg. I don't mind a camel's leg in my tent. What can it do? There's still plenty of space for me!" You should not think that.

By the time the night is over, you will find that there is an entire camel in your tent: head, neck, shoulders, all four legs and a tail.

You will find that the camel is in your tent and you, dear friend, will be sleeping outside.

don't let your ex get a foot in the door

Exes are special people: the kind you were sexually attracted to at one time and broke up with at one point or another. No matter how clean the breakup was, there are bound to be residual feelings. Seeing you happy with someone else might reactivate those feelings or lead your ex to feel like maybe something fundamental has changed about you. It has. You found the person for you. Don't let an old (crappy) relationship tempt you back. And don't make your best friend pull out all of that sad poetry you wrote to remind you WHY you don't want to go back.

If you are ready to get serious about a new person, you need to make a commitment, right here and right now, NEVER to go back to your ex. Don't wait for that awkward "why are you still talking to your ex" conversation, don't convince yourself that you and Charlotte the Harlot can still be friends, don't tell yourself that Timmy Two-Timer wasn't really that bad of a guy, just cut the ties and move on. If you can't, then you owe it to both yourself and this new person NOT to move forward. It's unfair to both of you to live in constant fear that the old relationship will rekindle, especially when this one's new.

there's no comparison

Because you read the first section of this book, you're now dating the best person for you...who could ever compare?

Don't compare your new relationship to your ex. Don't do it when you're mad....

"Oh my god you're acting just like my ex! That's why we broke up!"

Don't do it when you're sad.....
"This is the place I used to go for lunch with my ex. I miss him/her so much."

Do NOT do it when you're jealous or feeling insecure!

"My ex's boobs were bigger than yours."
"Oh that's your co-worker? He looks like the kind of loser my ex would date."

Just don't do it...promise?

If you want to get rid of someone, there are easier ways than to start spouting off about your ex. Nothing hurts more than ex spouting, either. STD's, no problem. You're homosexual now? Fine. Your ex? Nooooo!

Seven ex dont's
never, ever ever.......

1. Talk about your ex to your new lover unless it starts with "I hate" or ends with "was a total loser I never want to see again."

2. Hang out with your ex. You didn't break up because you were such good friends

3. Idolize the good times in your relationship and forget the fights, arguments, and of course, the breakup.

4. Put your ex on a pedestal.

5. Maintain a relationship. When it's done, it's done. Stop calling your ex's mom, unfriend them and their friends on social media, and avoid going places you know they'll be.

6. Rush directly into a new relationship. You're both going to get hurt.

7. Get stuck in denial. Is there a chance the two of you could ever get back together? No.

we are never, ever ever.......

18
MOVING ON IN

Ready or not, the two of you have started talking about moving in together. It has been months of hanging out, spending time, killing time, and wasting a whole bunch of money.

You've moved past the courting stage and into the next stage. Maybe you're excited! Maybe you're scared! Maybe you're petrified like you should have been in the last chapter when your ex was contacting you, that your freedom will be compromised!

How, you wonder, will you ever fart in bed again? What, you gasp, will you ever do with your porn collection? You're going to have to get a storage unit for those embarassing figurines you don't want the new partner to see! Maybe two storage units....

Putting a relationship spin on things really does seem to overcomplicate them for us. Moving in with a friend doesn't carry the same connotations and fears. When our best pal, confidant, and gaming buddy so close our usernames match wants to crash on the couch, all we do is set out a clean towel. Maybe.

Why is it that CrashSonic and SonicCrash can share a house, but Edwalinda can't? Because relationships are special. We can have multiple friends, hundreds of them... but it's taboo to have multiple relationships.

At some point, those cave ancestors of ours developed the good sense to understand that doing the mattress mambo exposes us to some very specific types of disease: the kind that are painful in our most tender areas. Now, our instincts tell us to pick one and settle down.

Our higher brains, those modern advances of ours, have different ideas. Why should we settle down? We have a job, a car, tons of friends, and we have STUFF. We don't want anybody touching our STUFF. Besides, we're already getting the sex. What the heck would we move in together for?

People have many reasons for moving in together. Some of them might be familiar, and others might surprise you.

it makes sense financially
Many couples are moving in together because, despite all of our whining that dating costs sooo much money, moving in together is a whole lot cheaper. Imagine splitting your household expenses in half. Welcome to the promised land.

physical and emotional support
It's nice to have someone around to help out. If you're not feeling well and need someone to do the chores you can't get done, that person is right there. You can share care for any pets, and lean on eachother emotionally when something goes wrong.

it strengthens the relationship
Moving in together is a commitment. For some couples, it is the first real commitment in their relationship. Moving in with another person tells them that they are the only one you want sleeping in your bed...or doing anything else in it.

you get to be lazy
No more planning dates, no more moving your schedule around. When you wake up, your partner is there. And at night when you go to bed? Still there! That promotion is in the bag now that you can focus on work!

so it must be time to move in together! but wait...

Many couples decide that moving in is not for them. In fact, some couples maintain relationships for years without ever living in the same house.

Will: We didn't live together until last year. My mother passed away and left me a condo, free and clear. We decided to take advantage of it together.

Steph: We moved in together sort of when college started. Our dorms are really close together.

Cameron: Meeting someone in college is kind of a cheat sheet anyway. Everybody's in and out of the dorms and student houses. You see the way people live.

Why do couples choose not to move in together? There are as many reasons as there are people. Don't move in if:

you feel manipulated
Feeling pressure from your partner is not a good enough reason to move in with that person. In fact, it could be a fantastic reason

to avoid moving in with that person. If someone is able to influence your decisions with a limited influence on your life, they're not going to be much less likely to make decisions for you when you're just on the other side of the bed.

you don't feel comfortable yet.
You have to feel pretty comfortable with a person in order to live with them. If you need to burp, fart, take a huge dump, or vomit all over the bathroom, chances are they're at least going to hear it. You may not want to destroy this person's image of you at this point in the relationship.

you're already fighting
If you're already having issues, moving in together isn't likely to repair them. Go back to chapter 14 and learn how to work it out before moving in together. If you aren't communicating well, it's time to take a step back and gain a little perspective before trying to live together.

you're hiding something
You're that person who looks at the floor when somebody asks what you're hiding, because it's true. It could be something as simple as grilling steaks at 2am...even in the

the middle of a snowstorm, or it could be something more complicated like all of the situations in part three of this book. Whatever it is, you don't feel comfortable enough with your partner yet to tell him or her. And hey, that's fine. If you don't want your partner to know that you wear a sleep apnea mask to bed or that you still have that rainbow brite doll from third grade, that's your business. And you can keep it your business if you want to.

you've seen the stats

Couples are moving in together more than ever. They call this a "trial period" to see if the relationship will work. Often, these relationships don't work out.

Viewing a relationship as something with a "trial" is a bad idea. First of all, it presents your partner as a business trying to sell you something. They are not. Your partner is a real person who, unlike Neflix after that free month, will become emotionally hurt if you decide heh, I don't really like the selection. It's amazing that we are so kind to shelter animals with notched ears and missing legs, but cannot show the same kindness to the people we claim to love, once they're in our homes.

we've decided to move in together... now what?

1. Set ground rules. Make a list of chores and decide who will do them. NEVER decide that the other person will do something: ask.

2. Make a list of items you will need for the new place, and items you both own. Talk about who will get rid of what and who will keep what. This is not something you want to argue over on your first day in a new place with movers charging by the hour. The decision making stage is the best time to figure this out, because nobody's moved out of their place yet.

3. Think about having a spare room, or finished basement. Right now if the two of you are arguing, one of you can just head home. That's not an option when two people are living together. It's important to have extra space that is your own, for those moments when you need to cool off. Or just be alone.

4. Decide on decor...together. Use the cash you'll save on rent or mortgage payments to buy new furniture and linens as a symbol of your new lives together.

the sh*t or get off the pot guide to proposing marriage

What? You're not married yet? Your mother had seven kids by your age. Your cousin has been married for five years. Your father had already moved out of your grandfather's house by the time grandpa was your age. Come on, we're not getting any younger.

Less couples than ever are getting married, and no one is sure why (least of all your grandma, who was expecting to be paying for a wedding dress by now). There are, however, more Pinterest wedding boards than there are wedding cakes in Rome, so it's pretty clear that people still want to get married.

As much as we tell ourselves that marriage is an archaic institution and a waste of time or energy, we love the idea of wearing fancy clothes, inviting our entire family, and throwing a huge party. Throwing our life long joy in the face of everyone who ever told us we'd never find happiness is just an added bonus.

What should you know before hiring a caterer and inviting all your exes?

get married because…

you love the person, not just the idea of having a wedding.

you can see yourself spending the rest of your life with this person. Picture yourself ten years older and still with them. what would it look like?

you love big parties, and making fun of your exes.

the idea of a wedding makes you feel great.

don't get married because…

you feel bullied into it.

you want to trap your partner

your partner makes more money than you, and this will force them to keep paying for your apartment if you leave

you're worried about your childbearing years running out.

you spent too much time on Pinterest this week, and thought those cakes looked tasty

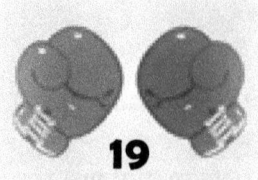

19

FANNING THE FLAME

Janice: People think the sex is going to fall off. For us, it's better than ever. I'm still so happy to see him when he comes home. I'm really happy to go to bed with him.

Cameron: I try to do little things for her every day. I bring home flowers or call her in the middle of the day to say I love her.

Steph: Send pictures to him on my phone.

Will: We have an ongoing date. No matter what else is going on, we get together every weekend and go to our favorite restaurant. She's a great girl, and I want her to know that.

Emily: I'll pay sometimes, take him out for his birthday. I write letters to him, so that he gets them in the mail. It's the little things.

You can become too comfortable with someone. Familiarity doesn't always breed contempt, but it can breed over-familiarity. It's important to remember why the person you are with fell in love with you in the first place. Doing things that remind them of who you both were when you first met can bring back the spark and those warm feelings you had for one another.

Without new reasons to appreciate the love you both share, your relationship can get into a rut or begin to taper off. You start to take eachother for granted and, in extreme cases, you may begin to look outside of your current relationship for the fulfillment you seek.

There are as many ways to rekindle a relationship as there are people in the world. This is the time to get creative and really focus on what makes you and your partner happy.

Think of your relationship as a new chapter in your life: one that will be spent with the person *you* chose. It's a very important choice. We don't get to choose many of our family members, and our friends tend to choose us, but relationships are chosen *by* us.

Your spouse will be the first family member you get to pick. Remember to choose your partner every single day, and don't let them go a day without knowing you love them.

ideas for a married date

1. Go to the place where you first met, and talk about your memories there. Bring a picnic lunch. Try to remember what you ate that first day.

2. Our memories are often triggered by scent, because our scent memories are the strongest. Wear the scent you wore when the two of you first met.

3. Plan an anniversary party. Have your family members compile photos from your relationship and have a toast...or a roast!

4. Go for a long walk (on the beach or, if you prefer, somewhere less cliche) and talk about your future together.

5. Splurge on a trip. Now that the two of you share a budget, why not put your income together and make a date...three or four months in the future.

6. Go on the date you wish had been your first. If your first date was a trip to the coffee shop in a beaten-up car, maybe it's time to re-write it. Rent a luxury car for the weekend and drive it to a beautiful hotel or cabin.

re-starting the conversation

You've been together for months or even years, and the conversation is getting stale. You've discussed the same memories from your childhood and ideas so many times that your lips are turning blue.

At the dinner table, you barely acknowledge eachother with a friendly nod. You used to have so many things to discuss, and now you always seem to know exactly what your partner is going to say.

If you're starting to feel like you've entered a time loop, it may be time to take the reins and re-connect with your partner.

According to our lazy research, there are six thousand (or so) movies and television shows on Netflix. There are billions of pages on today's internet, and something new happens on a global scale every single day.

People used to have a lot to talk about, but nowadays we tend to isolate ourselves in relationships. We no longer go out with friends, especially not the single ones; we spend less time with our families as individuals and more time as couples, and we're working so many hours that we can barely spend time with our partners, let alone the other people in our lives.

The only way to get out of your rut is to spend more time with the other adult people who matter to you. That way, the two of you have something to discuss when you finally do get time together.

If you're apart for a time, you will appreciate eachother more when you see eachother again. Make new friends, have awkward new conversations, and realize how important the comfort you share with one another truly is.

It's also important to carve out some time to be alone.

Cameron: I go to Fan Expo with a bunch of friends every year. Steph used to come along, and she hated it. Now I just go with my buddies. Our relationship is better than ever because she's comfortable enough with me to say "Hey, I don't want to go to…whatever thing you're going to."

Emily: Sometimes you just need a girl's night out, to have fun and howl at the moon.

do not, under any circumstances

There are a few really good ways to end even the strongest long-term relationship. If you want to destroy everything you've worked to build, we highly recommend:

1. Forgetting that your spouse is a person. Treating your spouse like a floor cleaner, dish washer, and/or pooper scooper is a great way to call it quits in the long run.

2. Being controlling or abusive. Maybe you didn't learn in the sandbox that hitting people is a bad idea. Well it is. If the two of you have frustration issues to work out, think about joining a gym.

3. Taking out all of your anger on your partner. Your boss won't leave you alone, your co-workers suck, and the traffic on the way home was a nightmare. What better idea is there than to come home and yell at your spouse, so that you can be alone forever?

4. Being disgusting. Use a kleenex, brush and wash your hair, and don't show your worst side to the person you are with. Over the years, you'll be etched in their long term memory as someone who grosses them out.

do looks matter?

It's been a long time, and by now the person you are with has seen you in every state. You've been up, you've been down, you may have even been covered in placenta. Why should you dress up, put on something that smells good, and try to impress them?

That depends how much you like the idea of your relationship lasting.

Wearing nice clothes, smelling good, and going out to show off shows your partner that you are still invested in the relationship. We all show our affection in different ways, but remember that a good relationship is usually based on mutual physical attraction. If there was no physical attraction, the two of you would just be friends.

Your personal appearance is the first thing that shows your partner that you still find them desirable.

Emily: It's not the fifties. I'm not going to put on my housedress and wash the kids' faces or whatever. But if he comes upstairs and I'm in lingerie, yeah, he gets the message that I still think he's a sexy beast.

little things that say "i love you"

1. Leaving a note in their lunch bag. Just because it reminds you of kindergarten doesn't mean they won't appreciate it. Especially if your note contains some very un-kindergarten like content. Buying lunch? Wrap it around a bill in their wallet.

2. Dust off a love cliche. Bring home flowers, give your partner a box of chocolate, or sprinkle flower petals on the bed. They're classics for a reason. Feel free to genderbend them with bacon roses or chips and beer.

3. Buy something for them. Save up to buy your partner that new power tool she's been drooling over, or get him that new pair of running shoes. Even if it's something they can buy for themselves, your partner will appreciate the gesture.

4. Don't forget to say "I love you." Just because you know it's true, doesn't mean they don't like hearing it sometimes.

5. Tell your partner how good he or she looks, or how much you're reminded of good memories when you see him or her. Don't skimp on the hugs and the kisses!

20
LITTLE BABY BUTTERBEAN

This is the final chapter of your relationship, and unless things get...interesting, you'll probably be leaving us now. Wookit our wittle bouncing baby butterbean all grown up!

Speaking of bouncing baby butterbeans, binkies, sippy cups, and potties, many couples will have children at some point in their relationship. Some also choose to opt out, and are happy going in that direction.

If having babies isn't your thing, we bid you adieu. If you are, however, interested in moving the needle on the Canadian birth rate meter (currently it's one child for every hundred couples, ouch!) then this chapter should arm you with information about bottles, soothers, spit up, freezing your eggs, the many uses for a thermometer, and all things baby related.

Whether you're expecting a baby, moving in with a single parent, or a veteran parent, these tips are for you!

are you ready for this?

Not every couple chooses to have a baby, but when you have the option, it's best to sit down together and really discuss the idea.

The biological imperative isn't enough to get you through eighteen years of everything from diaper changes to drivers licenses: for that, you're going to need a plan.

Not a comprehensive plan, since you don't know what kind of person your little butterbean will be until he or she gets a bit older, but at least a financial plan.

In the first year of life, tiny people can cost upwards of $10,000. Put aside an extra $500-$1000 a month while you're planning, and you'll already be off to a great start.

You're going to need a lot of support once the baby is born, especially if there are any issues. Don't assume that family members and friends will be there for you: ask them what role they plan to have in a potential child's life. Now is also a good time to have a health check. Tell your doctor about your plan and ask what you should do to prepare.

5 ways to tell if you're ovulating

1. Self check. When a woman is ovulating, she's very fertile. Understanding your usual sexual cycle can help you to figure out when you're ovulating. If the male in your life suddenly looks incredibly sexy and smells amazing, you may be ovulating. Or he might have worn the good cologne for once.

2. Take your basal body temperature (BBT) every day. Your body temperature increases 1/2 to 1 degree during ovulation. Without a thermometer, you wouldn't even notice the change. Yay science!

3. Use a tracking app. App stores and the web are full of free apps that can help you to track your periods, ovulation schedule, and other data related to periods and childbirth.

4. Watch your weight. Due to the buildup of tissues around a released egg, your weight may fluctuate by one to a few pounds during ovulation.

5. Try an ovulation test. Ovulation tests are expensive, but they're sold over the counter at most drug stores. They claim to be very accurate.

increase your chances

If you want to have a healthy pregnancy, you have to make the right choices. Some choices can take away from your healthy pregnancy and even keep you from getting pregnant in the first place.

proper nutrition

If you're thinking about having a baby, you've probably already heard that being over- or underweight can decrease your chances of getting pregnant. Doctors use your weight to determine your health, but that isn't the whole picture. Depending on your age, genetics, and the culture you grew up in, a "normal'" weight range might not be "normal" for you.

Taking in the proper vitamins and nutrients is more important than what you look like. The time to go on a diet is not when you're trying for or expecting a baby. Get rid of your fat and calorie tracking app, and use a vitamin and nutrient tracker like cronometer instead.

If you've got issues with eating properly, think about seeing a nutritionist for help.

toxic love
Living in a toxic environment isn't good for you or your baby. If you're living near a factory or glowing lake and it's feasible, you may want to consider moving. Certain household chemicals have also been known to decrease fertility, so do your research!

substance abuse
Smoking anything, including marijuana, can cause infertility and will harm a developing baby. Heavy drinking (more than 1-2 drinks a day) can cause infertility, and no amount of alcohol is safe in pregnancy.

physical issues
Certain conditions and even STD's can cause scarring on a woman's fallopian tubes or in her vagina. See a doctor to determine the physical issues that might effect your fertility.

stress
There's a reason why unwanted pregnancies are so common: when a woman is feeling happy, loved, and relaxed her body is more likely to get the baby engine running. Take up yoga, start meditating, and reconnect with your partner. Stay calm, enjoy life, and don't get so hung up on having a baby that you forget to spend time together.

the may/december lie

There is an interesting trend toward artificially limiting women's fertility in North America. Men are presented with an oddly idealized version of the facts, where they can have children until the age of eighty while women can't conceive past forty.

While it does conveniently normalize May/December relationships between older men and younger women, the theory does little else but make women feel as if they should be infertile at an early age.

Around the age of forty, when it's been well-publicized that women's fertility begins to fall off, men also experience a decrease in fertility. The quality of sperm also falls off, which makes pregnancy less likely and miscarriage much more likely.

Not surprisingly, in areas of the globe where exposure to these attitudes is less prevalent, women are much more likely to become pregnant at an advanced age. The oldest mother to conceive was 71 years old, and the next oldest was 66. Age mismatches are more about vanity (and delusion) than any kind of scientific fact.

medical intervention

Occasionally, medical intervention may be needed to help a couple get pregnant. There is so much cool stuff out there these days to help couples get pregnant faster, later in life, and with greater success. Check out these options while you're in the planning stages.

freezing stuff
More and more couples are freezing eggs and sperm for later use. Freezing eggs is also a great idea for young women who aren't yet considering pregnancy. What an awesome gift to your future self: healthy, youthful eggs ready to make one super baby!

in-vitro fertilization
In-vitro fertilization (or IVF) is what happens when a scientist takes out a petrie dish and inserts a sperm into an egg. Through science, we can create what the seventies lovingly called "test tube babies" which are then returned to the womb to become full-blown babies.

ongoing research
Cool things are happening every day. They're even close to finding a way for men to carry babies.

5 ways to prepare for parenthood

1. Set your alarm clock to wake you up every two hours to the sound of a screaming baby. Instead of setting your alarm clock to snooze, pick it up, rock it, wrap it in a blanket, and after 45 minutes, put it down for another hour and fifteen minutes. Make sure it goes off the second you start to fall asleep.

2. Have your spouse let out a blood-curdling scream every time you start eating. Ideally, this will be timed for the exact moment when you have the second spoonfull of food halfway to your mouth.

3. Simulate having a toddler by running up and down the stairs, trying to wedge yourself under things, bolting out the front door for no reason, and tripping over stuff. Don't forget to bark your shins and stub your toes as often as possible.

4. Pick up a copy of the player vs. player guide to parenting: Squid Pyjamas.

5. Talk to stoned,homeless people as often as possible. This will simulate conversation with children because they have strange opinions and no money. They will also puke on you.

PART THREE

RELATIONSHITS: HOW TO RECOGNIZE A BAD SITUATION, KNOW WHEN TO FIX IT, KNOW WHEN TO LEAVE, AND UNDERSTAND YOURSELF IN ANOTHER SUPER LONG TITLE

YOU'VE GOT TO KNOW WHEN TO HOLD EM, KNOW WHEN TO FOLD EM, KNOW WHEN TO WALK AWAY, KNOW WHEN TO RUN
-KENNY ROGERS

I'VE GOT A BLANK SPACE, BABY AND I'LL WRITE YOUR NAME
-TAYLOR SWIFT

SOME PEOPLE CLAIM THAT THERE'S A WOMAN TO BLAME
-JIMMY BUFFETT

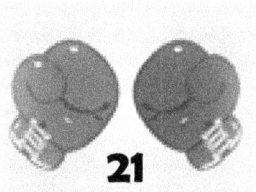

21

WOW...YOU REALLY PICKED A... LOSER

Not every relationship is going to be the perfect one for you, and some of them are going to completely suck. Not just a little bit. Not in that "meh, I really don't feel we should continue this" kind of way, but in a way that makes you wonder if this person is some kind of irritation professional with all of your hot buttons pre-programmed into their brain.

Before you know it, all of the flowers and candies, dinners and movies have devolved into arguments and yelling, door slamming and re-hashing of old fights. Don't you wish you'd known how to recognize the signs that are now so obvious, BEFORE you got into that relationship?

Luckily, some losers are universal. Avoiding them could be simple, if only there were a book that had an entire section devoted to the obvious signs that your relationship is now or will soon be in the junkyard under a car tire. And there is!

on the clock

This person makes you feel like you're always on the clock, and the clock is always running down. Dates feel a little like a scene from "Speed": you're always trying to finish fast, before this person runs out of time for you.

We all have lives, appointments, and conflicts in our schedule. Everybody gets sick or worse, runs out of clean laundry. The on the clock partner is always busy, and never has any time for you.

We make time for the things that matter to us. After a long day at work, all you can think about is spending a couple of hours with your partner, even if you're both half asleep in front of the TV set. All your partner can think about is spending a few hours at a shopping mall indulging in retail therapy.... maybe it's time to call it quits.

Hopefully before your new love is forgetting to pick up the kids from soccer practice.

At their worst, on the clock partners show up late at night and never stay over. This is the partner who comes over at 10pm and leaves at 2am, in one heck of a hurry.

the clingon

Not to be confused with those not-so-cuddly Star Trek characters, the clingon is someone who monopolizes all of your time. This person is the polar opposite of the on the clock partner.

At first, this person might feel like your best-ever partner. Attentive, loving, and over the moon obsessed with you. Who doesn't love a good ego fluffer?

You don't. Over time, the clingon becomes the very definition of crazy: stalking all of your social media profiles and commenting on every post, alienating you from friends and family, and manipulating every situation to be all about them.

"He called my ex boyfriend and told him to stay away from me."

"I told her that I needed to drive my kid to his concert. She cried and threatened to commit suicide if I didn't pick her up instead."

"At first, I liked the thought of being needed. That wore off pretty quickly."

have we met?

You've been together for four months, and things seem to be going along great. You've even met a few of your partner's friends. But whenever the two of you are out in public and especially if you run into people, this person drops your hand like a hot potato and whistles like you're two strangers holding the same strap on the TTC.

The have we met? partner might be the best human on earth behind closed doors, but that doesn't matter when they're introducing you to "old friends" with some platitude (if they introduce you at all).

"I found out at the border. The border guard asked 'what are you to eachother?' and he said 'we're just friends'. We had been dating for six months. I was so crushed."

"We were walking down the street holding hands, and she randomly just dropped my hand. Then she'd run up and hug some old friend of hers."

"We'd be out together and my boyfriend would physically wedge himself between me and the other person. I couldn't even talk."

noncommital

Can you imagine your future together? Spending long summer days on the porch, watching your grandkids play in the yard. Swimming in the ocean, hanging out on a yacht, retiring and working on your garden?

This person can't.

Your partner can't even commit to pizza toppings, and definitely isn't in this for the long run. When you talk about being official, they turn into a glassy-eyed doll staring through you. You'll talk about it later, and later never comes.

Whether it's month six and this person still isn't officially dating you, or year six and they "hadn't thought about" moving in together, it might be time to, as Chris O' Donnel so famoously said in 'The Bachelor', "Shit or get off the pot."

"He told me that if we were still together in seven years, we'd get married. Year seven rolled around and he said he'd forgotten. And it was probably just some stupid thing he said anyway. Apparently the relationship was some stupid thing I did."

so much in love...with their ex

I want to date someone who is still in love with their ex...said nobody ever.

This partner was usually the dumpee in their last relationship, and hasn't quite gotten over it. Even if they were the dumper, the way they talk about the ex makes you wonder if the ex shot out butt rainbows every time they had sex.

This person is always looking for their next ex. They enjoy being miserable, and need someone to blame. You're never going to mean anything to this partner...at least not until you break up and YOU become the problem in their next relationship.

"He was very defensive of his ex. If I said she wasn't that pretty, he'd jump down my throat and literally yell at me."

"Lisa, her ex, could do no wrong. It didn't matter if I helped her with car payments, took her out for dinner, bought her flowers... nothing I did was good enough."

"Every time his ex called saying she needed him, he ran out the door."

do you really have to cheat?

This person is constantly trying to make you miserable, and pushing all of their buttons. You've been known to say things like "I think he's cheating, and if I find out it's true, I'm kicking him out."

The do I really? partner doesn't really have to cheat in order to make you miserable. Ask yourself how cheating would really change the way you feel about the relatinship. It probably wouldn't.

When we have made up our mind to leave someone, some of us will sit them down and tell them honestly that we don't see any future. Some of us become passive aggressive, and start deliberately messing everything up.

"My ex boyfriend used to complain about the dishes not being done, and if the house wasn't perfect. By the end of our relationship he was smoking and putting out his smokes on the couch. My whole couch was full of cigarette butts. It was pretty clear he hated me, but I kept telling myself he still loved me if he didn't cheat."

"It was obvious that she hated me."

i want, therefore you are

This person is a freaking wizard. Watch them wave their magic wand and feel the shock and amazement as they call you into existence...only when they need you!

Never calling you just to say hello, this person only wants you around when you can provide some product or service for them. You only exist when they need a ride somewhere, need something paid for, or want a free meal.

Hey, can you come over to take a look at their car? They really need someone to hook up their computer. Maybe you can babysit later?

"She only called me when she needed a ride somewhere. We had sex less than once a month, and it felt like an obligation."

"He was always flirting with other guys. There was no respect. I felt like I was his chauffer, taking him to parties so that he could find someone else to talk with. "

"I'd take her to a club or a show and she'd ignore me. She wasn't really my girlfriend."

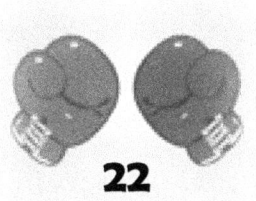

22

TAPPING THE MAT

Nobody wants to give up on a relationship. When things start to go south, most people don't give up right away. You have feelings for this person, or you wouldn't have chosen to be with them in the first place. You might even have shared property and small tokens that remind you of eachother.

When is it time to tap the mat, throw in the towel, and give up on trying? When have things broken down so far that they can no longer be fixed?

"The breakup is the worst part. I practically write down what went wrong with the last one hoping that the next one will have whatever magical traits the one I'm leaving didn't have. So the breakup won't happen this time. I hope."

"My parents were together for fifty years, but they were miserable my entire life. My dad lived like a tenant in my basement, and I almost never saw him. I felt strongly that he didn't love me, or any of us really."

paint a picture

Make a list, write a journal entry, draw a picture, or create a dream board with "my best life ever" printed at the top. In your dream, where is your partner?

When you look at that photo of a woman parasailing, the wind blowing through her hair and her freedom level at 200%, do you imagine a man beside her on his own parasail, smiling alongside her? Or do you picture him back on the beach, hitting on the bartender and creeping out vacationers' daughters?

When you imagine yourself as a star athlete raking in millions, do you imagine your girlfriend sitting up in the stands cheering you on and blowing kisses, sending you the wink that wins the event? Or is she sitting at home with drugs piled on the table, waiting for you to show up and give her more cash?

If you can't picture a future that has your partner in it, it's probably time to move on. Ultimately, you should be with someone who you can see yourself spending a lifetime with. If there are disagreements now, they probably won't get better over time.

can we talk?

Every relationship has the occasional communication breakdown, and the tips in chapter 14 can help as long as the arguing isn't frequent and extremely distressing.

Frequent arguments about the same things mean that you have fundamental differences that can't be resolved. When they finally do break down, there's never a resolution: just a fuming silence while you wait for the next argument to start up.

Often, the arguments are based on a bigger, underlying issue. Maybe one of you was unfaithful. Maybe one of you wants children and the other one doesn't. Whatever it is, you know that conversation about it goes nowhere.

Each smaller argument becomes a substitute for the bigger problem. Over time, communication breaks down to the extent that you kind of feel like a scientist trying to explain quantum physics to a toddler. When did this person you used to love become so stupid? Why can't they understand a simple concept?

Because the love is gone, my friend.

the dollhouse complex

Everything seems fine from the outside. It's all exactly the way it used to be. Same sheets, same blankets, same pillows.

This morning before work, though, you noticed that the life had drained out. When you woke up, your partner felt like a giant doll lying beside you. You were civil to eachother, but something was missing.

When the food tastes like plastic and the air feels suffocating, you begin to become exhausted. Before long, your once loving home feels like a dollhouse: plastic walls ready to be knocked down.

"I just knew that I was living in a house of cards. When he told me that he was cheating, it wasn't like he knocked the cards over. It was more like they had already fallen, but I didn't know it yet."

"It was a cushion cover. I know it's crazy, but we got this cover when we moved into the house. It had two little lovebirds that had always reminded me of us. I looked at it, and I just saw a couple of birds. I started crying long before I told him it was over. I knew."

post-apocalypse

You've been with the same person for so long that you're convinced walking outside the door will put you in a post-apocalyptic world. You've survived such a relationship war that it's obvious (to you and nobody else in your life) that there is nobody else out there for you.

If you're only staying because you're afraid of being alone, it's time to go.

Since this situation is more likely than any other to result in cheating, you need to take responsibility and leave before anything like that has a chance to happen.

Sure, you've known this person for a long time, and might even have begun to think of your partner as a family member.

Remember, though, that your partner isn't just someone you trade pleasantries with at birthday parties and gifts with at Christmas.

A fear of being alone, or of not being able to find anyone better, is not a good enough reason to stay together. You know that, and your partner probably does, too.

empowerment is sexy

We are our own worst critics, and that's why your partner should always be your biggesst cheerleader. A partner is someone who lifts you up when you're feeling down, and always believes in you...even when you don't.

A good partner might become critical, but only when you're selling yourself short or getting yourself into a bad situation.

If you're feeling weakened or disempowered by your relationship, it's time to go. You have goals, and you know where you're going in life. You need a partner who lets you drive the bus, and even takes the wheel when you no longer feel motivated.

When someone disempowers or belittles you, they're putting up a red flag. You may not even be aware of it, but somewhere in the back of your head, a feeling will start to grow that this is someone who doesn't like you very much.

"You get the feeling that nothing you do is good enough for this person, and when they say they love you, or even like you, it just seems like empty sounds."

the agreement is ended

No-one likes to think of a relationship as a contract between two people, but it is. The two of you agreed on something going into this, and one of you has broken the contract. If you agreed to be faithful and one of you cheated, agreed to have children and one of you is suddenly disinterested, or agreed to share the household expenses and one of you isn't holding up their end of the bargain, it's time to call it quits.

You can't trust someone who doesn't keep their promises. Maybe your partner didn't mean to lie to you; your partner might have been very serious when the promise was made. Over time, though, something broke down. If you can't live with the new contract between you, it's time to pack up and leave.

infidelity

In the special case of infidelity, the person who was cheated on will often try to stay with the cheater. This hardly ever works, and usually ends up with the faithful partner being called a liar down the line when he or she gives up on trying to make things work. Sometimes you try, and nothing works.

please don't go....

"It's for the best". Leaving because you think your partner would be happier without you works against itself: your partner won't be happy, because you're gone. If you have a major illness, permanent disability, just found out that you're infertile, or anything else has happened to convince you that your partner would be better off without you, don't leave. A good partner would rather support you through this than know you are suffering alone.

In a good relationship, either partner can feel like they aren't good enough. When you love someone, you will tend to put them up on a pedestal. As Bryan Adams said; "When a man loves a woman she can do no wrong. He'll turn his back on his best friend if he puts her down."

Never leave someone because of negative feelings about yourself, unless you have done something that is hurting your partner. If you have been unfaithful, have a drug habit, or have physically assaulted your partner, then you should leave to protect that person from yourself. That said, don't martyr the relationship because of low self esteem.

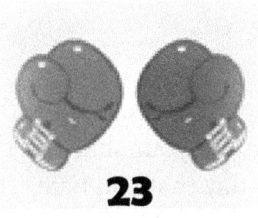

23

HOW TO BREAK IT OFF

"We were in this relationship that just wouldn't end. I felt like I had broken up with her a thousand times, and she just wasn't listening."

"We lived together, so it was one thing to call it over. It was another thing to figure out our finances and everything else."

Maybe you've already broken up with someone, and maybe you're trying to figure out how it's done. Either way, breakups are a messy business, and they almost never go well.

Even if you both already know it's over, one of you is bound to be hurt by this. The one being broken up with will always have a harder time of it: they tend to be the one who gets all of the sympathy from family and friends.

In fact, some skilled manipulators will let the relationship continue for a very long time, trying to get you to break up with them. They'll get under your skin and do the little things every day that you hate. They are likely to seem even MORE distressed than the average person being broken up with, because they love the attention they're going to get from family and friends when they paint you as the guilty party.

That said, most people who have been in a relationship with you aren't trying to manipulate you. They have just been caught in a different stage of the relationship than you're in.

If you're thinking about breaking up with someone, you've probably already gone through the stages of trying to work it out, hoping things get better, and telling yourself that you can make this last.

When you break up with someone, they are probably still in one of those stages. Just as your internal narrative tells you it's time to break things off, that person could be looking at YOU and thinking everything's going to be fine. They might even have had a plan in mind, a picture of the two of you working things out and living hapilly ever after. Be sensitive to that and take it slow.

don't go ghost

There is only one right way to break up with someone. You need to make sure they know they've been broken up with. It might be easier for you to just stop talking to them, but it's not easier for the other person.

ghosting makes you look like a douche

in person? maybe....

Most experts will tell you that breaking up in person is the honorable thing to do. You know your relationship and how it works. Some breakups need to happen in person, others can be accomplished via text message.

As a general rule, end the relationship the way it started.

The way your relationship started can be a great yardstick for determining how to end it, because it gives you a clue to the way the person you're with likes to deal with nerve-wracking or uncomfortable situations.

If you met online and it took them months of talking to you to be able to meet you, then they're probably not the kind of person who wants to be publicly humiliated at a restaurant in the middle of a workday.

If you break up in person, don't do it in public.

This should go without saying, but many of us still decide to break up in a public place so the other person won't cause a scene. You just broke up with this person! A scene is going to happen, and breaking up in public means you just caused the scene to happen in front of a crowd. Possibly even a crowd full of people they know. Not okay.

don't text it.

The main reason never to break up over dm, text message, or any other messaging service is that the person can't be sure it's really you.

"My boyfriend was in the shower, and his buddy got ahold of us phone. He started texting me that we were breaking up, and I believed it was my boyfriend so I blocked him from my phone. It took him three weeks to get ahold of me through other people. His buddy thought it was hilarious but neither one of us was laughing.

never involve a third party.

Don't bring a friend to your breakup, unless there was violence in the relationship. If you are worried about violence, call the police to escort you rather than going alone. Do not EVER, under ANY circumstances, bring a date to your breakup. I don't care how much you hate him, I don't care how much she hurt you, don't do it. Ever.

a false hope

It's important to make a clean break, rather than allowing the person to think that they might get you back if they try hard enough. If there is nothing the person can do to get you back, just say that. Be firm, but polite.

Cut off any sexual commentary or touching immediately. Don't tell the person they can be your friend, or that the two of you will still do things together, especially if it isn't true.

You may think you're being nice and sparing your partner's feelings, but let's face it: you're not. What you're doing is actually cruel. It keeps your partner from being able to find someone new, for one thing.

False hope is self-serving. It fills a need in you and drags down your partner. You get to have your cake (a new relationship) and eat it too (you don't have to worry about being alone if it doesn't work out).

Meanwhile, your partner is spending so much time striving to get you back that he or she has no time to move on and start a new life without you.

i want my t-shirt back

If you know you're going to break up with someone, it can be a good idea to prepare. Usually a breakup has been coming on for a long time, so rather than running through scenarios in your head, trying to figure out what to say and how to say it, try to figure out what will remind the person of you, and how to remove it.

Now is the time to start taking down tags from social media, and removing any photos that might be tagged with their name and have you or both of you in them. If you find something of yours in their room, take it out. Box up and even throw out items you bought together, and start deciding who the dog is going to live with.

Your partner is probably not going to be able to think about this practically: they're going to be feeling hurt and distraught. As the person planning the breakup, you're going to have to step up and minimize their suffering by keeping the reminders out of their space.

When you split, the person may ask to keep something of yours. Whether you allow this is up to you. Can they heal if they have it?

never ever ever do this...

1. Make it their fault. Maybe if they had tried harder you wouldn't be ending it...so if they change something you won't leave? Be honest. There's nothing they can do and no, you're not coming back.

2. Blame someone else. They need their friends and family for support, so don't throw a friend or family member, especially one they're very close with, under the bus.

3. Rehash old grudges and arguments. This is you ending the relationship, and that means you're done with all of the arguments that brought you to this point in the first place.

4. Agree to stay friends. You have no idea whether a friendship is going to be possible between the two of you yet, and it's best to just say that.

5. Try to get others "on your side". You've had the same friends for a long time, and now they feel like they have to choose sides. Make sure everyone knows where they stand, and never tell anyone to stop hanging out with your ex.

24
ONE MAN'S TRASH

Unless you're a complete psychopath, you're probably going to feel really bad for the person you're breaking it off with. When you break up with someone, they're very likely to have a strong emotional reaction. They might be angry, crying, or defeated.

Seeing someone you love or once loved like that really hurts, especially if you've tried hard to make it work. Most of us aren't monsters who enjoy seeing someone else in pain. We're people, who once loved the person we're now breaking it off with.

It's hard for anyone to believe that the person breaking up with them still cares, but it's the truth. You care about them, but you no longer have feelings of romantic love for them.

When you tell your ex that he or she deserves better, the odds are that you mean it. The odds are even better that your new ex doesn't believe it.

the perfect person for them

When you know it's over but refuse to break it off with someone, or keep giving someone false hope, you are damaging your ex. As much as you might think you're being a good person and making things easier, the truth is that you're not.

You're making it harder. And to be honest, you're not being a good person, either. You're being a scared person who wants a backup plan in case this one fails. You're being an insecure person who can't imagine your ex moving on from fantastic, wonderful you.

A good person doesn't want to make someone else suffer. There's a difference between paying lip service to wanting better for your ex, and helping your ex to move on.

This is where we separate the emotionally mature from, as the kindergardeners say, the "giant diaper babies". When you break up with someone, it gives them the opportunity to find someone new. Someone better for them.

One day, you'll have to watch your ex being happy without you. Be happy for them.

why couldn't i be the one?

It's hard to break up with someone, and even harder to see them happy later, because we want to be the one they're compatible with.

"I just wanted my ex to find work. After he left me, he ended up finding a great job. All I could think was that if I'd waited a little longer, we would have been fine."

Chasing your own happiness is easy, but seeing your ex happy with someone else can be much more difficult. Suddenly, remorse sets in and you realize that you can never go back.

Worse than buyer's remorse and a food coma combined is the feeling that maybe you were wrong in leaving your ex. Your ex isn't empty box from ebay or a bad clam, but a person. With real feelings.

To make matters worse, your ex might find someone new right when your relationship is ending.

DON'T try to get your ex back. Stay strong. Remember why you broke up in the first place, and don't give in to missing them.

i'm total garbage

Every day, somewhere in the world, someone is guilted into a relationship with someone they can't stand. The person might be less than attractive to them physically, mentally, or in many other ways.

How do they end up together? Why is Schlomo Johnson dating the high school cheerleader while Sexy McHotterson strikes out?

There's an obvious answer: money.

The obvious answer is wrong. Normally, in relationships where one parter is much more attractive (barring an honest-to-god fetish) a combination of guilt and low self esteem play a role.

"I wasn't attracted to him sexually or any other kind of way. But he showed up crying because no girl wanted him. I just felt bad for him. I cheated on him all the time and he didn't even care. It was so sad."

You should never date someone just because they cried, whined, or begged. Someone who does these things might be honestly feeling sad, but they're most often trying to push the situation over in their favor.

You're not hurting someone by turning them down. You're helping them, as well as the people around them who they're refusing to see.

"My best friend for the longest time was a guy. I really liked him but he acted like I was invisible. He always talked about how he was so in love with this girl or that girl. They were all really pretty but none of them ever liked him. It made me really sad that he would take being alone forever thinking about them over being with me."

You might also end up stuck in a relationship with someone you normally wouldn't date because of your own self esteem issues.

"I dated guys who were a lot bigger than me because it made me feel like one of the little skinny girls I wanted to be."

If you're with someone just because you don't want to seem mean or superficial, remember that they are also superficial. They are trying for the best possible partner, and you should do exactly the same thing.

personality conflicts

A relationship that was terrible for you might be good for someone else, especially if you and your partner were using different ideas and your own language to describe the world.

It's been said before in this book and it bears repeating: not everyone was born in the same community or in the same family.

Sometimes relationships fail because of basic personality conflicts. Genuine differences in your moral structure. Thought processes that don't match up.

Sure, the fun you have together (and the sex) and the movies you like watching (and the sex) and the friends you share (and the sex) might be good enough that you can ignore the fact that one of you is a slob and the other is a neat freak, or that one of you is a Christian and the other is a Wiccan, or that one of you is a type A and the other is a slacker...

but eventually the person you really are inside will win. You won't be able to stay with someone who is the opposite of your ideal.

the caregiver

There are people who seek out individuals who are sick or injured in order to take care of them. They have a desire to feel loved and wanted by being with someone who is dependant on them.

It's never good to get into a relationship because the other person needs you. Whether the need is real or fake, you are not seeing your partner as an adult human being and someone to love.

"Speaking as someone who has been in a wheelchair yeah, there are people who want to date you because of the chair. I just want to be a person to them. See me first, not the wheelchair."

You are not responsible for saving your partner. Things happen in relationships, and you might be called on to help your partner physically at some point. That's fine, but don't baby your partner or seek out someone who needs (or is willing to pretend to need) your help.

Disabled and injured people are still people: see the person first and the injury second.

my mama don't like you...

Just because you don't like someone, doesn't mean nobody else will. Just because you broke up with them, doesn't mean they have to be alone forever. Never treat someone like they are irrelevant, garbage, or don't matter.

Don't insult your ex or bring up their flaws when you leave. don't say stupid things like:

"You can't really blame me for hitting on your best friend. Her boobs were bigger."

"Maybe if you hadn't gained weight, I would still want you."

"You should have gotten a job. Then we'd still be together."

They usually come from your own feelings of inadequacy and have nothing to do with your partner. These are the kind of statments you make when you're trying to hurt someone...as if breaking up with them weren't enough.

No matter what issues you had when you were in the relationship, don't go out of your way to hurt your ex when breaking up.

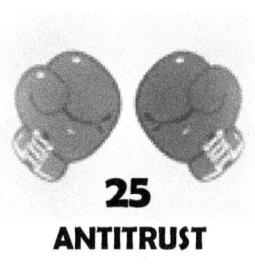

25
ANTITRUST

Antitrust is a government practice that keeps businesses from forming monopolies. Don't say this book never taught you anything. The obvious benefit is that the marketplace is kept free and we pay a fair price for goods and services. Nobody will start charging $1000 a bottle for water and killing off anyone who can't afford it.

Ironically, this is the same thing we do to destroy the trust in our relationships: keep ourselves open and available to others, and never quite put our hearts where our mouth is.

Peter Hoeg wrote, in Smilla's sense of snow, that "In every deep and abiding love grows a hatred toward the beloved, who now holds the only existing key to happiness"

You're just being smart, and making sure that nobody has a chance to hurt you. Sure, nobody can get close to you either, and you spend long periods of time alone, but that's a small price to pay..isn't it?

cheating abuse and control, oh my!

Unfaithfulness and abuse (on the facing page) are the two worst things you can do to your partner. They violate a trust between yourself and your partner and are usually the result of your own insecurities.

knowing why you do it might help you to stop.

Experts and internet trolls have a lot of ideas about why people cheat, most of them focused on the person being cheated on. Two things are obvious: that experts play to the person who wants answers, and that the person who wants answers is usually the cheatee, not the cheater.

Telling people who have been cheated on how to recognize a cheater and how not to get cheated on gives cheaters attention, and that's what they crave. Incidentally, it also tells them what not to do if they want to avoid getting caught.

If you are a cheater, the only way to stop is to understand that not everyone is like you. You're not cheating on your partner before they get the chance to hurt you.

Abuse comes from the same place as does cheating: a fear that your partner is better or more capable of leaving than you are, and a need for control.

The victim is never the issue in an abusive home. Most often, the abuser has been in a situation where he or she felt extremely weak in the past. They might have been abused themselves, or had it modelled to them.

In some families, negative behavior is normalized. Kids are allowed to play fight or run around with guns beating on eachother. Parents hit their children or break their belongings to get back at them for not doing a chore. Their children bring a lot of anger and resentment with them to school, and learn that they can control others through violence.

The only person who can stop abuse from happening in a relationship is the abuser. The only person who can stop cheating is the cheater.

Although they play out differently, both situations come from the same place: an idea that everyone is a terrible person, and you're "winning" by being the worst of the bad.

trust issues

People with trust issues tend to be broken up with a lot. No matter how much the other person trusts them, it's never enough. They feed on trust and go out of their way to test the boundaries of their relationships, and this leads to a lot of breakups.

"The way he acted, it was like he wanted us to break up."

"She seemed to really enjoy being miserable. There was nothing I could do or say to convince her that I wasn't going to leave her. When I finally did leave, she was like 'hah'! I told you! Well no kidding. I'm not going to stick around and keep being treated like crap just to prove to you I'm better than your other boyfriends."

Even if you have trouble trusting people keep it to yourself

Don't use your lack of trust to manipulate others. Act as if you trust them, and don't look for information to the contrary. Allow them to have private access to their own cell phones and accounts on the computer, and don't ask why they came home late.

But...how will you ever catch anyone cheating?

Simple. Cheating isn't about sex, it's about control. If it were just about sex, the cheater would tell you they were doing it. In fact, many polygamous couples have done just that and been very successful in their lifestyle choices.

There are two components to cheating: having sex with someone else, and hiding it from you. Cheaters get off on hiding from people who are looking for them, because their goal is to get caught.

It doesn't seem to make sense, but the cheater is the happiest when he or she is caught. They're addicted to having the upper hand and having a lot of people completely head over heels obsessed with them.

Obsesed enough to yell at eachother? Great. Obsessed enough to get into a fist fight? Even better.

Having a trusting spouse is no fun for the cheater. They get bored quickly when you refuse to stalk their social media, stare at their phone, or follow them around.

who cares if your partner is cheating?

A lot of people type "how can I tell if my boyfriend/girlfriend is cheating?" into search bars and forums every day. So how many cheaters are there in the world?

In the 90's, there were a lot. Remember the study in 1992 that found 75% of married men and 70% of married women had cheated on their spouses?

Which is why the answer most given by experts, on forums, and in chat rooms is usually "if you think someone is cheating they probably are".

Then again, you probably are as well.

Most accusations of cheating don't come from non-cheaters: they come from fellow cheaters hoping to throw shade on the cheating partner before it's cast on them. Let's face it, to the victor go the spoils, and the cheater is much less likely to keep friends and family members (and beloved dogs) than the cheatee.

Still, let's assume you're innocent, and truly

worried your partner might be cheating.

All of the signs are there: your partner is pulling away from you emotionally, spending a ridiculous amount of time "at work", abusing substances, hanging out with random people of your gender and calling them "friends".... but always has to hang out with them alone....

Why do you need this person to cheat before you break up with them? All of those signs don't need to point to cheating in order to be unloving and miserymaking. If you're picking up on a feeling that someone really doesn't like you, then it's time to run.

"He was always disappearing and spending huge amounts of money. I figured he must have another girl on the side."

Whether or not he has another girl on the side, he disappears and spends huge amounts of money. He could be secretly maintaining a horse ranch and it would still be taking chunks of money out of your pocket.

Who cares if your girlfriend is stepping out, if she's posting half naked pictures of herself all over the place and partying without you?

you played yourself

Paranoia is a great way to end a relationship. Make sure that your ideas are based in reality and don't let the fear of losing control you.

It's normal to get ideas in your head when you're in a relationship. New relationships in particular are scary: you live in fear that this new and amazing person is going to ghost you, or leave you, or stalk you, or worse!

What isn't normal is looking through their cell phone, smelling their clothes hoping to find evidence of cheating, and making wild accusations.

Sometimes, things that go wrong in relationship happen in our own minds. When that happens, thing can turn sour very quickly if we don't recognize what is happening.

Whenever you feel like arguing with your partner,, ask yourself if they really did what you think they did. Are you reacting to something that actually happened, or is emotion clouding your judgement and leading you to believe that they said something they actually didn't say?

26
JUST GET OVER IT

Whether you were the dumper or the dumpee, getting over your ex isn't as easy as the people who are sick of hearing you talk about getting dumped make it sound.

In order to heal from this and move forward without damaging your next relationship, though, you need to find a way to get past whatever went wrong.

This last chapter is dedicated to getting over heartbreak, and it's as short as we hope your hearbreak will be.

Before you read it, here's a band aid.

Hopefully, it helps. At least a bit.

don't let anyone tell you how to feel

After a break up, you might feel angry, stressed, hurt, relieved, exhausted...

you might also feel that people are irritated by constantly having to hear you complain, and they probably are. And that's okay.

They're your feelings, you are entitled to them, and you're the one who had to listen to them whine the last time they got broken up with, so the least they can do is sit there and take it.

it's okay to wallow

It's okay to dig yourself deep into a well of sadness. In fact, your next relationship may not work out very well if you don't. Bury the feelings you're having now, and they're only going to pop up later.

If you don't hate on that evil slattern for her cheating ways now, you're going to be upset and paranoid that the next girl is cheating on you later.

Write your miserable poetry, lock yourself in a dark room, and be sad if you want to.

it's okay to hate yourself

Some of our greatest personal growth is accomplished in those moments where we truly hate ourselves. It sounds counter-intuitive, but you aren't going to hate yourself forever. Take these moments of being angry with yourself as a learning experience. Don't just beat yourself over the head with "I'm a loser" and "I suck"...think about what went wrong, and how you could do things differently the next time.

this won't last forever

In the moment, it might seem like you're going to be miserable, hurting, and in pain forever. You might even want to feel like crap forever. It would serve that jerk who hurt you right. No matter what, please remember that you are going to heal from this. One day, soon, you're going to look back on this moment and think, look at that person.

In that moment, remember that strength doesn't come from refusing to care. It comes from finding the power to care despite having been hurt in the past. Few of us marry our first love. Don't bring your bad experiences with you.

take care of yourself

1. Go back to the things you enjoyed doing before you were in a relationship.

2. Do the things you stopped doing in the relationship that annoyed the hell out of your partner. Come on, we know you want to!

3. Take a class.

4. Volunteer.

5. Spend time re-connecting with friends and family, especially the ones your partner hated. You can gripe about them together.

6. Don't get too hateful. Fixating on being angry at your ex isn't going to help you heal.

7. Try not to make contact until you're fully over this. Talking to your ex can be painful in the beginning stages.

8. Don't stalk your ex. Seriously, don't look at any social media posts, don't ask mutual friends how they're doing, don't even think about going past their house. Make your life all about you for awhile, and ignore that jerk who didn't know how great you are.

get back out there

Even if you're not feeling ready to date again, it can be good to go out on a few easy dates just to test the waters.

Get up, get dressed, and leave the house. Flirt shamelessly, and remember that there are still people in the world who think you are wonderful, charming, and sexy.

When you're ready to go out and have a great time again, flip back to the beginning of this book to start finding the perfect person for YOU.

Thanks for Reading, for stepping up, and for being brave!

www.ingramcontent.com/pod-product-compliance
Lightning Source LLC
Chambersburg PA
CBHW061429040426
42450CB00007B/963